D0522171

A LOAD OF BLAIR

JAMIE WHYTE

A LOAD OF BLAIR

CORVO

First published in Great Britain in 2005 by
Corvo Books Ltd.
64 Duncan Terrace
London, N1 8AG

A catalogue record for this book is available from the
British Library.

Jacket design by Henrietta Molinaro & Richard
Roberts.
Author photograph by Tom Garside.
The speech 'Choice, Excellence and Equality' is repro-
duced by permission of 10 Downing Street.
Typeset by SJM Design.

Printed and bound in Great Britain by Cromwell Press
Ltd., Wiltshire.

ISBN: 0-9543255-5-9

For Zainab

CONTENTS

Preface

Politicians have a bad reputation for misleading the public. People think they are liars.

Perhaps some of them are. But lying is only one way of misleading people. Improper reasoning is another, and it is much more common than out and out lying. If a politician's logic is wonky, then even if he begins his rhetorical journey on the firm ground of truth he will probably end it in a swamp of error. And, if he manages to carry people along with him, then he will have misled them, whether he intended to or not.

Voters need a nose for bad logic as well as bad faith. This book is intended to help develop the required olfactory ability. It proceeds by identifying the fallacies common in political rhetoric and then holding samples close to the reader's nose so that their smell may become familiar.

Some will think the enterprise naïve and misguided. Political rhetoric, they will say, is not about truth and logic; it is about winning over the audience by any effective means, rational or not. It probably is. But the objection mistakes my target audience. This is not a manual for politicians: 'How to beguile the public.' It is for the benefit of voters: 'How to resist the beguilers.' The fact that politicians attempt to win our support by means other than rational argument is precisely what motivates the book.

Most of the examples of bad reasoning are drawn from the rhetorical output of the Prime Minister. This may seem unfair on Mr Blair; his predilection for bogus arguments does not distinguish him among politicians. But, as our teachers always told us, the fact that all the children do it is no excuse. And there are, in any event, special reasons to focus on Mr Blair's rhetoric.

The most obvious is simply the amount of it. Over recent years we have heard far more from Mr Blair than from any other politician. Leaders of the opposition and cabinet ministers have come and gone while Mr Blair has remained in place, chatting to us almost incessantly. Only the chancellor, Gordon Brown, has stayed the course, but he is the strong silent type.

More important, however, is the fact that Mr Blair's rhetoric is distinctively modern and very successful. Mr Blair is the model for a new, empathetic, all-things-to-all-men style of communication. It has helped him lead the Labour Party to two general election victories and probably to a third in the spring or summer of this year. Politicians from across the political spectrum and around the world have sought to imitate his style.

A classical education is conducted by studying the masters. When all the wisdom of the ages is distilled in the works of a mere handful of great men, why waste time on the minor figures? This book concerns the opposite of wisdom, but the rationale for focusing on the works of just one man is much the same.

PART I
Love Me!

I used to work as a management consultant. My first project manager gave me some advice: your clients need not like you, they need only value your advice. Quite right, I thought. Our clients are spending vast sums of shareholders' money on consulting projects. Their duty is to make sure they hire the best consultants, not the most likeable.

Then I noticed that one of my firm's most successful and sought-after directors was one of the least able. In fact, he had a strong tendency to talk nonsense. But he was charming: handsome, bonhomous and full of boyish confidence that everything was going brilliantly. Many clients adored him. They would pay his exorbitant fees simply to have him around.

That is not what they told themselves, of course, nor those to whom they had to justify their spending. They let their attraction to the man convince them that, really, he was a brilliant consultant who offered valuable advice. And he encouraged them in this delusion, mixing work and friendship into a heady cocktail.

Politicians attempt similar trickery with voters. They try to make themselves attractive to us in all sorts of ways that have nothing to do with whether they have the best policies or will be competent in the roles they seek. They work to convince us that they are virtuous or fashionable or well intentioned or, in a bizarre twist of democracy, just ordinary, run-of-the-mill people. And by mixing this self-characterisation in with their plans for government, they hope their likeability will somehow rub off on their policies. If you think I am a good bloke, you must think my policies are good too.

Few British politicians try as hard as Mr Blair to win us over personally. We get good Tony: Christian, family man and global visionary who holds forth on the moral dimension of his domestic and foreign policy. We get cool Britannic Tony: guitar playing, pop-star entertaining, football supporter who goes on holiday in the mansions of billionaire friends. And we get sentimental Tony, who emotes with us about the pain of loss, from Princess Diana to his own youthful good looks.

Perhaps Mr Blair is right in his estimation of the modern British sensibility. Perhaps this posturing generally inspires affection rather than nausea. But even if it does, no one should cast his vote on the basis of such affection. I love my mother, but if she ran for parliament I wouldn't vote for her. She has a muddled set of political ideas and the wrong temperament for dealing with crises. Affection is irrelevant. You don't have to like the person you vote for; you need only think he will do a better job than his rivals will.

The following chapters deal with three ways of trying to inspire irrelevant affection in the electorate. All politicians indulge in them to some degree but few show Mr Blair's dedication.

1 Good Intentions

Young men often try to impress young women with tales of their future achievements. She may not realise it, but she is being chatted up by a soon-to-be Arsenal striker, millionaire investment banker or world's greatest poet. Catch the train before it leaves the platform baby!

Sensible young women are unimpressed by such declarations. Desiring fame and wealth does not distinguish a young man. What matters is the likelihood that this desire will be fulfilled. That is one of the attractions of men who are already rich: all doubt on the issue is eliminated.

Voters should be equally unimpressed when they hear a politician stating his ambitions for the country. He may genuinely want to make Britain the most peaceful, prosperous and just nation on earth. But that will not distinguish him from his rivals, who almost certainly have the same ambitions. Only if a politician has unusual goals is it interesting to hear about them. If, for example, he seeks to maximise our chances of going to heaven then that might be worth knowing about. It would incline him to make very different decisions from a politician who sought only to improve our lives here on Earth. But if a politician aims for all the usual stuff – opportunity for all, high quality education, the ability to walk safely on the streets and so on – then we should skip directly to how all this is going to be achieved.

Yet politicians rarely do skip straight to the interesting part. They prefer to spend quite some time laying out their vision for the nation. In the 2001 Labour Party manifesto, for example, Mr Blair listed his government's goals for 2010:

1. Long-term economic stability
2. Rising living standards for all
3. Expanded higher education as we raise standards in secondary schools
4. A healthier nation with fast treatment, free at the point of use
5. Full employment in every region
6. Opportunity for all children, security for all pensioners
7. A modern criminal justice system
8. Strong and accountable local government
9. British ideas leading a reformed and enlarged Europe
10. Global poverty and climate change tackled

Beginners in specifying political goals ought to study this list well. It is a beautiful example. First, there are ten goals. Ten is really the only suitable number of goals. Not only is it a round number, it is likely to bring to mind the Ten Commandments with all its divine authority. Seven, though also biblical, might conjure up the deadly sins and so should be avoided. Twelve is OK, what with the twelve disciples and all that, but the number has been tainted by the Alcoholics Anonymous twelve step recovery programme. You don't want to cast Britain as a recovering alcoholic.

If you feel there are more than ten things you need to mention, don't worry. Do what Mr Blair does and simply combine two into a single goal, like 'opportunity for all children, sec urity for all pensioners'.

Note also the date for these goals to come true: 2010. In 2001 that was nine years away. Nine years is not so far in the future that people will consider the goals irrelevant. Goals for 2050 would look silly. But 2010 is still far enough away that no one will monitor progress too closely. And by 2010 you can be confident that these goals from 2001 will have been forgotten altogether.

Then there are the goals themselves. Most present no serious risk of failure. Sometimes this is because they are almost guaranteed to be realised, however inept the government. Living standards, for example, have risen under every government since the Second World War; it would be astonishing if they were not still rising in 2010. More often, however, the detection of failure is made impossible by the vagueness of the goal. How will we be able to tell if the justice system in 2010 is modern? Or if the government has tackled global poverty? Metaphorical ambitions are easily achieved.

What makes this list of ambitions truly worthless to voters, however, is the fact that it does not distinguish the Labour Party from the Conservatives or the Liberal Democrats. Not one ambition on this list would be rejected by any of Mr Blair's rivals. Does Mr Blair expect voters to believe that the Conservatives seek insecurity for pensioners, economic instability or declining living standards for all?

*

Declaring such obvious ambitions fails a simple test for substance in a statement: namely, that someone sane might disagree. Anything that would immediately win the agreement of anyone but a lunatic can be taken for granted. It should, literally, go without saying. But it rarely does in Mr Blair's rhetoric, which is padded thick with such banalities, and not only when discussing his 'vision for Britain'.

The principles he espouses also tend to be so obvious as to be empty. In 1997, for example, he informed an audience that:

> For all my adult life I have kept to some simple be-
> liefs – that people achieve more together than they
> can alone. That the rights we enjoy are matched by
> the duties we owe, that security is life's most pre-
> cious commodity.[1]

The belief that people can achieve more together than alone is, as Mr Blair says, simple. So simple that it is not worth mentioning. No one would deny it: not a Marxist nor a *laissez-faire* capitalist nor anyone in between. Anyone looking for reasons to support Mr Blair's policy agenda can only find such platitudes worthless.

Mr Blair may have principles that are more than mere plat-itudes. For that very reason, however, we are unlikely to hear about them. A politician does not tell voters about his prin-ciples so that they might know the basis on which he will make difficult policy choices. Such principles – ideas from economics, jurisprudence and so on – are difficult to articu-late and far from guaranteed to win the agreement of most voters. Keep it trivial: that's the trick.

In January 2004, shortly after becoming leader of the Conservative Party, Michael Howard published a personal creed of sixteen principles. Sixteen is a strange number of principles; for reasons already considered, it should have been ten. And in the case of Mr Howard's principles ten would also have had the virtue of reducing their number. For they are pathetic. None distinguishes Mr Howard from Mr Blair or from Gordon Brown or, indeed, from anyone who can operate a toaster. They include the following astounding ideas:

> I believe that people must have every opportunity to fulfil their potential.

> I believe in equality of opportunity. Injustice makes us angry.

> I do not believe that one person's sickness is made worse by another's health.

It is reassuring that Mr Howard does not believe that good health causes illness. But there must be many crazy things he does not believe. Why did he mention this one? My guess is that he is hinting at a more interesting idea: that stopping the wealthy from buying private medical treatment will not make the poor any healthier. He does not simply say this because, unlike his empty platitude, it isn't indisputably true. If you taxed the wealthy to the point where they could no longer afford private medical care, and spent all that money on medicine for the poor, then maybe you could make the poor healthier by making the rich sicker.

Politicians hate to get caught saying something false. But they ought to take the risk. By saying only what no one could possibly deny, they fail to say anything interesting at all. It may be easy on the ear and the brain but, as far as giving voters useful information goes, they might as well recite the phone book.

Most factual errors in modern political speeches come not from the risk inherent in making interestingly unobvious assertions but from rhetorical over-exuberance. After announcing his intention to make Britain a decent society, Mr Blair declared:

>The truth is you can only feel good – are only entitled to feel good – in a decent society: a society where the rules are fair; where everyone has a chance; where people co-operate as well as compete; a society where government is on the side of all the people and not just the few.[2]

This is a gloriously noble sentiment but is it really the truth? Is it even what Mr Blair really believes? Can he think of no indecent society where people feel good? How about Fiji? It has a racist constitution that requires a majority of parliamentary seats to be occupied by ethnic Fijians. This is not a society whose rules Mr Blair would consider fair. But it is apparent to anyone who visits Fiji for even a few days that many people there feel good, and with no apparent lack of entitlement.

The claim that people can feel good, or are entitled to, only in a decent society is obvious nonsense. But it is pious nonsense. And that is the kind of nonsense people like, as any preacher or new age guru will be able to tell you.

When the rhetoric gets highfalutin, watch out. It is likely to be either trivially true or obviously false. Many in the audience will enjoy being swept along by the tide of sanctimony. But they should not be deluded. However enjoyable the ride, it is not a journey of discovery. All these visions, principles and simple beliefs contain no information that could help anyone sensibly to cast his vote.

*

Most politicians waste our time with platitudinous, visionary waffle. But few are as ambitious or as glib as Mr Blair. No problem is so difficult that it cannot be dissolved by his moral purpose. In his speech to the 2001 Labour Party conference he declared his intention to save the world:

We can't do it all, neither can the Americans. But, you know, the power of the international community could, together, if it chose to. It could, with our help, sort out the blight that is the continuing conflict in the Democratic Republic of the Congo ...We could defeat climate change, if we chose to. Kyoto is right. We will implement it and call upon all other nations to do so. But it's only a start. With imagination, we could use or find the technologies that create energy without destroying our planet, we could provide work and trade without deforestation ... And if we wanted to, we could breathe new life into the Middle East peace process, and we must.

The *Daily Telegraph* called this speech 'Blair's finest hour' and in *The Daily Express*, Romesh Ratnesar said it was 'the most cogent, rigorous, and stirring oration of his or any other current British politician's career'.[3] Yet the idea that the world's largest problems would disappear if only people really wanted to solve them is adolescent piffle. The Middle East peace process, for example, has received decades of well-intended attention. Nevertheless, the situation has mainly worsened. Unless Mr Blair has some specific idea about how to improve things it is not very interesting to be informed that he cares. Anyone can care, and anyone can say he does.

2 Good Me

> I know it's hard for people to keep faith. Some of the
> people may have a different take on me. But I have
> the same take on them. I trust their decency. I trust
> their innate good sense. I know I am the same person
> I always was, older, tougher, more experienced, but
> basically the same person believing the same things.

Mr Blair made these remarks during his 2003 Labour
Party conference speech. He was defending his decision to invade Iraq. He also had something to say about his
physical appearance. He believed that, at fifty, he now looked
his age and that after six years in power he was 'more battered without but stronger within'.

Many commentators claimed to be moved by these revela-
tions: tears were apparently shed around the nation. Some of
us, however, were moved in a different direction. Boris
Johnson captured our feelings in his *Daily Telegraph* column:

> How dare this mincing poodlefaker stand up and start
> confiding to the nation about his emotional journey

of the past six years? We don't want to know whether you think you look older, you big girl's blouse. We want to know what plans you have to improve the lot of the British electorate.

Invading Iraq may have been a good idea. Perhaps it will liberate the people of Iraq, reduce the threat of terrorism and stabilise the Middle East. If Mr Blair could show that these are its likely effects, he would have a good case for his action.

His personal morality, however, is irrelevant. Suppose we accepted Mr Blair's high opinion of himself, that he is generous in his opinion of others, steadfast in his beliefs and strong within. How does any of this show that invading Iraq was a good idea?

When it comes to assessing a policy, the personal morality of those who support it is neither here nor there. They may be fine people with good intentions, but the policy may be stupid for all that. The virtuous are not immune from error. Nor are the wicked always wrong. Who was the more virtuous man, Neville Chamberlain or Winston Churchill? You needn't answer that question to know who had the better policy for dealing with Hitler's military expansion.

Despite its irrelevance, Mr Blair rarely misses an opportunity to let us know how good he is. His 2003 party conference speech was not out of character. Right from the start his speeches have been chock-a-block with moral posturing. Shortly before Labour's 1997 electoral victory, for example, Mr Blair assured us that:

> The health of the family and the strength of the nation ultimately reflect the quality of honest, decent, truthful government, government which has a moral dimension and which always makes sure that justice has a high place at the Cabinet table.[4]

Like so many of Mr Blair's statements, this is almost incomprehensible. What does it mean to say that the health of the family depends on the honesty of the government? What does any of this tell us about the policies Mr Blair might pursue or why they will work? To look for such meaning, however, is to misunderstand the statement's purpose. It is only supposed to create a certain impression: namely, that Mr Blair is honest, decent, truthful and just.

*

Mr Blair led the Labour party to victory in 1997 persistently telling us that we could trust him. Ever since, trust has been a dominating theme in British politics. Indeed, many commentators tell us that there is now a 'crisis of trust'. After their reprehensible conduct in the 1990s we still do not trust the Tories, but we have also lost our trust in Mr Blair. People are now considering trusting the Liberal Democrats.

Trust does have an important role in politics, but it should not hold the primary position that modern politicians and journalists give it.

When deciding whether to vote for someone you must try to predict what he will do if elected. He may tell you what he plans to do, and you may agree with these plans, but that isn't enough. Like other people, politicians do not always do what they say they will. Before voting for a politician you need to believe both that he honestly intends to do what he says and also that he has the strength of character and competence to get it done.

That is why trust is important in politics, and also why it comes a clear second to policy. Only when you support a politician's declared policy agenda should you care if he can be relied upon to implement it. If you think his policies are wrong, the issue of trust doesn't arise. You might even prefer him to be dishonest or weak-willed.

Mr Blair's rhetoric, however, tends to suggest that trust is the first issue, policy the second. We ought not quibble about his policies but simply put our faith in Mr Blair himself. If he is good, then his policies must be good too. We ought to 'keep faith'.

Perhaps he got this idea from the Bible. According to *Romans* 8:28: 'All things work together to good for them that love Jesus.' And who can doubt that Mr Blair loves Jesus? Alas, biblical origins do not much increase the chance of an idea's being true. The idea that everything will work out well for the virtuous is ridiculous.

So is thinking that people should trust you because you say you are trustworthy. Claiming to be virtuous is not very strong evidence that you really are. On the contrary, it is grounds for suspicion. When a used car salesman begins a sentence with 'honestly, guv, ...' you know what to think of what follows. Trust is something you must earn through your behaviour. When people don't trust you, begging them to is unlikely to help.

*

Voters need not be overly concerned by the morality of a politician. Provided we can trust him to stick to his declared policy agenda, and not to mislead us about information to which he has privileged access, it should make no difference to us if he is an adulterous, child-beating, dog-kicking bastard. It might matter to his wife, children and pets but that is their problem, not ours.

It may seem that trusting politicians to be honest about their policy agenda, and about what they really know, requires us to make a moral assessment of them. But it doesn't. Or, at least, it shouldn't. To see why not, consider the trust required in science.

Suppose we discovered that the author of a scientific

article in *Nature* was morally reprehensible. Suppose he committed the crime that most often gets politicians fired for gross moral turpitude: he had an affair with his lab assistant and lied about it to his wife and head of department. We would not change our view of his article. We would not claim that, since the man is a liar, his alleged findings cannot be trusted. The rigour of modern science means we need not worry about the honesty of scientists. Fabricating evidence is so likely to be found out and so severely punished that self-interest alone stops scientists from doing it, even when they are adulterous liars.

Any system that depends on the superior morality of its participants is poorly designed. A well-run army does not require heroic soldiers, and a well-structured polity does not require honest politicians. Political deceit should be so readily discovered and punished that even the most conniving politician becomes utterly trustworthy.

Our present system approximates this ideal, as illustrated by Mr Blair's trials regarding the accuracy of his claims about the military threat posed by Iraq. The controversy shows both that trust is important in politics and also that personal morality is not required to secure it. The tenacity of the press in pursuing a scandal means that any self-serving politician is well advised to stick to the truth. Since we can rely on the system to keep politicians honest, we need not care if their innate decency is also up to the task.

The system currently fails, however, in one important area. When the opposition is more or less unelectable and the press has become too cynical to take the offence seriously, politicians may break election promises with impunity.

In the 2001 Labour Party manifesto, Mr Blair promised: 'We will not introduce "top up" fees and have introduced legislation to prevent them.'[5] In January 2004 he successfully passed legislation introducing top-up fees.

In 2002 the Labour government increased National

Insurance from 9% to 10% and removed the cap whereby it is paid only up to the top rate of tax. National Insurance is now also levied at 1% on all income above the top rate threshold. These changes were exactly the same as increasing the basic and top rates of income tax by 1%. Yet in the 2001 Labour Party manifesto Mr Blair pledged he would 'not raise the basic or top rates of income tax in the next parliament'.[6]

Since Mr Blair is as close to moral perfection as can be expected from a politician, we clearly need some external discipline to make politicians keep their promises. In business, this discipline is provided by the fact that cheats will be sued for breach of contract. That is surely the answer in politics. Voters should be able to sue parties or politicians who break election promises. Those parents whose post-tax incomes have dropped while their children's university fees have risen should be able to sue Mr Blair for their losses. That would teach him to peddle a false agenda. And the threat of it would keep other politicians honest too.

Politicians will claim that breaking their promises was forced upon them by unforeseen circumstances. Sometimes this is true and, when it is, it will provide an adequate defence in court. But it isn't always true. No such excuse exists in either of the above cases. The university funding pressures that motivated Mr Blair to introduce top-up fees were well known at the time of writing his 2001 manifesto. And so were the increases in government spending which required the one percent increase in income tax. Indeed, they were advertised in the manifesto itself.

The main result of giving voters this redress against dishonest politicians would be a dramatic reduction in the number of election promises. But that would be nothing to regret. Which do you prefer: twenty empty promises or one serious promise? Or even no promises at all? No information is better than disinformation.

3 Good Company

On a summer's morning in 1992 about 600 fellows of Cambridge colleges gathered at the university's Senate House to vote on an issue that had received a surprising amount of media attention. Should the French philosopher, Jacques Derrida, receive an honorary degree? I thought he shouldn't and I sat myself down on the 'no' side of the room.

As I waited for everyone to get seated and counted, I couldn't help but notice that all the beautiful women were on the other side of the room. (There are not many beautiful women amongst Cambridge fellows and they are easily noticed.) Indeed, the other side of the room was generally more appealing than mine: younger, cooler, better dressed. If I hadn't been so convinced that Derrida was an intellectual disaster area, I might have made a last minute dash across the floor.

Everyone wants to associate himself with the cool crowd, or at least with his idea of the cool crowd. Many of the old 'bachelor dons' seated around me were probably glad to be on the tweedy side of the room. It's a harmless urge when nothing else is at stake, as is usually the case when advertisers exploit it. All those beautiful, young, half-naked people having so much fun with their Coca-Cola. If that makes you want to drink Coke, or if the desire to 'just do it' makes you want to buy Nike shoes, you haven't necessarily made a mistake. If you think Coke will make you more beautiful or Nike shoes will make you physically fit, you have gone wrong. But that is not how these ads work. The advertiser says, 'This is what my product represents,' and by buying it you say, 'Me too.'

Not everything, however, is as unimportant as which brand of consumer good you buy. It would have been stupid and corrupt of me to vote for Derrida because I preferred the look of the other side. There was a real issue at stake, regarding which the aesthetic appeal of the opposing camps was irrelevant.

The same is true in politics. Political parties may acquire an image, either by accident or intentionally, and you may or may not care for it. But, insofar as these images are not derived from the parties' policies or the calibre of their personnel, they are irrelevant to which you should prefer. The images don't help to predict which will do the best job in government.

Nevertheless, modern political parties work assiduously to cultivate an appealing image. They hope that you will be drawn to them in the same way that you are drawn to Coke or to Nike or to any of the other successful brands – not because you have any reason to think that they have the best policies or people but just because you want to associate yourself with the appealing crowd.

In the United States, political campaigning resembles the low end of the entertainment industry. Indeed, it involves many of the same people, not only running as candidates but lending their celebrity endorsements. American political party conventions have an aesthetic somewhere between professional wrestling, TV evangelism and a village fair.

None of this would go down well in Britain. Even given the

great progress of British sentimentality, American political campaigning still strikes most of us as gauche. But that doesn't mean British politicians do not indulge in the same shenanigans. They simply employ a style better suited to British sensibilities. Irrelevant associations needn't be boldly declared in red, white and blue; they can be subtly suggested just as well.

*

In the early and mid-1990s British art and pop music enjoyed a revival in popularity. Artists such as Damien Hirst and Tracey Emin gave us 'Brit-Art' and bands such as Oasis and Blur gave us 'Brit-Pop'. The fabulously successful Spice Girls were self-consciously British, with Ginger Spice even substituting a small Union Jack for a dress.

The artistic output of these cultural icons was of dubious merit. But even if you think that Britain should be proud of Tracey Emin's bed or the Spice Girls' telling us what they really really wanted, it all had nothing to do with the Labour Party. This revival of British pop-culture occurred during John Major's premiership.

Nevertheless, Mr Blair went out of his way to associate himself with 'Cool Britannia'. He courted media and business celebrities in a way that had never before been seen in British politics. He seemed to be a close friend of everyone who was then cool, from Noel Gallagher to Richard Branson. In 1997, he threw a party at Number 10 to which he invited his Cool Britannic friends. Absolutely everyone was there.

At the same time that Britannia became cool, football also went through a revival in popularity. 'New Lads' like football. Television money flooded into the sport and newspapers devoted ever more pages to it. And Mr Blair announced his abiding interest in football. He was frequently to be seen on television having a little knock about. Poor old John Major was burdened with a genuine passion and talent for cricket, which is not a cool sport at all.

The English national football team is, alas, inclined to disappoint. The English rugby team, however, won the World Cup in 2003. Mr Blair, it turned out, had always been terribly keen on rugby. There is nothing that he will not glob onto if it makes the people of Britain happy.

Or sad. Mr Blair's great triumph of irrelevant association was appropriating Princess Diana to the Labour Party. He achieved this in a speech on the day her death was announced. The chin wobbling was helpful, but the master stroke was dubbing her the People's Princess. The Labour Party is the People's Party. People's Princess, People's Party. Get it?

In matters of style, it is hard to deny the association. Like New Labour, Princess Diana was friendly with many celebrities, obsessed with her public image and openly sentimental. But these qualities, though debatably attractive in a Princess, are no reason to vote for a political party.

*

It isn't only celebrities and sports with which Mr Blair likes to associate himself. He also keeps company with the greats of political history, at least rhetorically. Here too, he covers all the bases. Just as he can call on football or rugby according to the needs of the moment, so he has both the Capitalist Margaret Thatcher and the Socialist Aneurin Bevan on his team. He is the Real Madrid of politics.

In the mid-1990s, when Mr Blair was trying to convince the electorate that he was no longer the extreme left-winger he had been in the 1980s, he liked to associate himself with Margaret Thatcher. He let it be known that he admired her.

All those Tories who were disaffected by John Major's government but still adored Margaret Thatcher should vote for her natural successor, Mr Blair. And many of them did.

Mr Blair's problems have changed since he was elected. Nowadays he struggles to convince people that he is any kind of Socialist at all, let alone an extreme one. When it is important to be a Socialist, at Labour Party conferences for example, Mr Blair calls upon Aneurin Bevan, founder of the National Health Service (NHS) and hero of the Left.

Most on the Left of the Labour Party disagree with Mr Blair's plans to extend consumer choice and the role of private companies in the public services. So, in June 2004, Mr Blair explained to them that it is what Aneurin Bevan would have wanted:

> Aneurin Bevan said the NHS civilized the country. It extended choice, quality and opportunity in its generation: it didn't limit them. And when it came to means rather than ends, Bevan was entirely pragmatic about how provision should be funded and structured within the new NHS, consistent with its values of equality and fairness.[7]

When confronted with difficult decisions, many American Christians ask themselves, 'What would Jesus do?' To show his Christian credentials during the 2000 presidential campaign, Al Gore let himself be filmed with an inspirational *What Would Jesus Do?* plaque on his desk. It makes the skin crawl but you can see the sense in it for a believer. Jesus was omniscient and morally perfect. Do what He would do and you can't go wrong.

Nye Bevan may have been a great man, but he was not divine: even his most ardent fan would not claim infallibility for him. Asking yourself what Nye Bevan would do is not a sure path to righteousness. No one with good reason to doubt the merit of Mr Blair's policy should change his view simply upon hearing about Mr Bevan's posthumous support for it. Especially when it is not clear how Mr Blair knows what he would have thought of it. Bevan was pragmatic; my policy is pragmatic. It's not a great argument.

Perhaps, however, Mr Blair has more direct access to Mr Bevan's opinions. Death need not be an obstacle to the tenacious advice seeker. Mr Blair's friend Hilary Clinton has drawn on the wisdom of Eleanor Roosevelt in brainstorming sessions with people who can conjure up the dead.[8] And Mrs Blair has apparently received considerable information from 'the other side', channelled through one of her spiritual advisers, Sylvia Caplin.[9] 'Are you there Aneurin? Knock twice if you support Foundation Hospitals.'

The Blairs should be more open about their eccentric religious beliefs. It may create some trouble for them in the Catholic church, which still believes that talking to the dead is bad form, but think of the potential for celebrity endorsements. Noel Gallagher is all very well but he pales to insignificance compared to what the whole of British history has to offer. 'Vote Labour. Shakespeare Would.'

PART II
Magic Words

Istill remember my confusion when first asked, 'What's the magic word?' I was attending a friend's birthday party and his mother was making receipt of a piece of cake conditional on hearing this special sound. The only magic word I knew was from *Ali Baba and the Forty Thieves*. As it turned out, 'open sesame' was not what Mrs Bullen wanted to hear. All the well trained little bastards sat there stuffing their faces while I received a sermon on the perils of being smart.

I have since learned that if you are to get what you want in life, you are well advised to use language in the appropriate way. If you want to be an archbishop, for example, it won't do to swear and shout. Such language is for aspiring pop stars and investment bankers. Archbishops should speak in a hushed and beseeching tone, and what they say should indicate excruciating moral sincerity.

If you want to be a prime minister, or simply a member of parliament, you must also learn the proper use of language.

Tone of delivery may vary, within limits. You can be strident when the occasion calls for it, though you must not go so far that anyone could describe you as ranting. Measured and thoughtful has its merits too, provided it does not slip into intellectual and boring. Whatever style you choose, however, you must stick to one important rule. You must not speak plainly. If you do, people will know what you mean. And that can be disastrous for a politician. It makes it too easy for voters to discover that they do not agree with you.

Yet nor should you bewilder people. Voters must feel they understand. You must appear to speak plainly. And your plain words must be chosen so that they please almost everyone, whatever they believe. You must speak in a way that promotes not understanding but agreement. That's the trick.

Magicians' tricks are spoiled by knowing how they work. The gasps of amazement are replaced by yawns. The same goes, I hope, for politicians' tricks. The following chapters reveal three ways politicians use language to win our agreement without making it clear what we are agreeing with. If voters were wise to them, the head nodding and applause these tricks now induce would quickly be replaced by eye rolling and groans of impatience.

4 Double Meaning

In June 2003, Scott Sullivan, former Chief Financial Officer of the telecoms company WorldCom, was charged with defrauding the company's creditors. He was accused of misrepresenting the financial strength of WorldCom by describing the firm's operating costs as investments. An investment is a one-off expenditure used to acquire or build something that it is hoped will generate future profits. Costs are the ongoing expenses associated with doing business, such as paying power bills and staff salaries. Whereas costs are deducted from revenues to calculate a company's operating profit, investments are not. Categorising costs as investments thus overstates a company's profits. That was Mr Sullivan's crime.

It is fortunate for Mr Blair that politicians are not as easily prosecuted for defrauding the electorate. He has been perpetrating the same misrepresentation for several years now. He consistently refers to government spending as investment. In his 2004 Labour Party conference speech, for example, he described the billions of pounds of government spending on extra nurses as 'year on year investment' in the health service.

The expression 'year on year investment' is oxymoronic. Investments are not year on year: costs are. The expense of building a hospital or school may fairly be described as an investment. Paying the salaries of thousands of new nurses and teachers may not; their salaries must be paid every year.

Why does Mr Blair refer to all government spending as investment? I can't be sure; I don't know Mr Blair, nor therefore what motivates him. But I suspect that he likes the positive connotations of investment. Government spending is apt to be wasteful. Government spending reminds people of the tax that funds it, so that increasing it does not necessarily please them. Investment, on the other hand, sounds like something that will be rewarded with future dividends. Spending is wasteful and indulgent; investment is wise and visionary.

Despite investment's good reputation, it is not always wise. If it were, buying shares would be a guaranteed path to wealth and no company could ever go wrong by expanding. Nor is all government spending wasteful. Or, even if it is, it may still be justified. The judicial system, for example, may involve waste but it doesn't follow from this that we would be better off with a privatised judiciary. Government spending can sometimes be defended. Mr Blair presumably thinks that his policy of massively increased government spending on health and education is an example.

Alas, properly defending the policy is not easy. It would require Mr Blair to engage with issues that are both difficult and dull: the connection between competition and efficiency, queuing versus pricing as a mechanism for allocating a scarce resource, that kind of thing. And who knows if the argument would run his way? Better to give the whole business a swerve and defend the spending by simply calling it investment. Who could possibly object to investment in health and education?

*

During New Zealand's 1985 public debate on the proposed legalisation of homosexuality, the expression 'anal intercourse' came into popular currency, because it aided clarity. Whereas 'homosexuality' is ambiguous between certain sexual acts and a man's disposition to be attracted to other men, 'anal intercourse' is not. I heard a caller to a talk-radio show, however, who was not impressed. 'Call it what you like,' she declared, 'it's still sodomy!' You see, political issues are not so difficult; call things by their proper names and the answer is evident.

Politicians like Mr Blair also believe they can dispense with proper argument and rely instead on the judicious use of terminology. They systematically use words with strong positive or negative connotations to describe things whose virtues or vices are hotly disputed – as though, since we are here talking about 'investment', 'terrorism' or 'drug-pushing', there can really be no question on the matter.

The absurdity of this ploy is obvious. Even if you agree that all investment is good or that all terrorism is bad, there is still something to dispute: namely, whether the activities in question really are investments or terrorism.

People who seek victory through terminology attempt to take advantage of an ambiguity inherent in many words with evaluative connotations. 'Sodomy' is a good example. It has a non-evaluative sense, in which it simply refers to anal intercourse. Anyone who engages in anal intercourse thereby engages in sodomy. However, 'sodomy' also suggests that the act is sinful. The term comes from the biblical story where God destroys the cities of Sodom and Gomorrah because he doesn't care for their residents' habits, including anal intercourse. In the United States, sodomy laws are those that make certain sexual acts illegal, including oral sex in some states.

There are, in effect, two meanings of the word 'sodomy': anal intercourse and morally wrong sexual act. The talk-radio caller I mentioned above tried to take advantage of this fact to make the following argument:

1. Anal intercourse is sodomy (by definition)
2. Sodomy is morally wrong (by definition)
3. Therefore, anal intercourse is morally wrong.

If this argument were sound, we could deduce from the meanings of words alone that anal intercourse is morally wrong, which we obviously cannot. The appearance of success comes from the fact that the word 'sodomy' is used with different meanings in premise 1 and premise 2. The argument commits the fallacy of *equivocation*.

The talk-radio caller took advantage of, or may have been genuinely confused by, a real ambiguity in the word 'sodomy' to make her specious argument. Alas, the modern political equivocator cannot depend on the availability of a relevant and ambiguous word. That is why he must often indulge in a little linguistic innovation: that is, make up new meanings for words. To take advantage of the positive connotations of investment, Mr Blair simply starts calling government spending investment, as though it were up to him what words mean. His implied argument runs:

1. Spending more on nurses is an investment (by new usage of A. Blair, PM)
2. Investments are wise (by popular misunderstanding)
3. Therefore, spending more on nurses is wise.

Insofar as we accept Mr Blair's new meaning for the word

'investment', we should no longer be willing to agree with premise 2. Even if real investments were always wise, that would tell us nothing about investments on Mr Blair's new definition: blinvestments, let's call them. The fact that we like investment is irrelevant when assessing the merits of a blinvestment.

The trick works just as well when disapproval is sought. Simply call the object of disapproval by the name of something that you know everyone hates. Terrorism is the most obvious example. Mr Blair now refers to almost any aggression against Western interests as terrorism. Even those who fight soldiers occupying their country are called terrorists. You may agree that the invasion of Iraq was a good idea and that no Iraqi should resist it. But it does not follow from this that those who do resist are terrorists. Nor does calling them terrorists prove that they are wrong to resist. That requires proper argument, not simple name-calling.

Terrorism is such an obvious case of this trick that it doesn't work. If everybody notices your extended usage, you are likely to encounter linguistic resistance. The debate about the rights and wrongs of any military action is these days a debate about whether it can properly be called terrorism. But an unexpected or bizarre piece of linguistic sleight of hand can still work wonders.

Before the 1997 general election, Mr Blair denounced the Conservatives; after eighteen years of Tory government, a third of British children lived in poverty.[10] Shocking, isn't it? In a country as wealthy as Britain in 1997, a third of children lived in families too poor to provide adequate food, clothing, housing, medical care or education for their children.

Shocking and also impossible to believe. The poorest in Britain are the unemployed. The state provides them with free housing, education, healthcare and enough cash to buy basic food and clothing. Most own or rent fridges, ovens, telephones, televisions and even cars. All this was as true in 1997 as it is today. What does it mean to say that they live in poverty?

What Mr Blair means is that they live in households with incomes less than 60% of the national median household income. A third of children live in such households, so a third live in poverty. In the academic literature, a distinction is drawn between absolute and relative poverty. Going without nutritious food, housing and healthcare is absolute poverty: the kind of thing many in the developing world suffer. In countries like England, where few suffer absolute poverty, people can still suffer relative poverty; they are poor compared to other people in England. At best, Mr Blair's statistical definition of poverty is a definition of relative poverty.

But he never mentions this in his speeches. He simply claims that a third of children live in poverty, plain and simple. Most people will assume he is talking about absolute poverty. Why should people who have never even heard of relative poverty assume anything else? And Mr Blair benefits from the misunderstanding, because his implied argument requires it.

He claims that we should support the Labour Party's policies aimed at fighting poverty. Why? Because poverty is dreadful and there is so much of it. But this is just a play on words. Absolute poverty is dreadful, but rare. Relative poverty is common, but not so dreadful. When the relatively poor are not absolutely poor it is more difficult to make the case for fighting poverty. And who wants to engage in difficult arguments? Better to simply fudge the difference between relative and absolute poverty and let our abhorrence of the latter do its work.

*

On the 24th of September 2002, when preparing the nation to

go to war with Iraq, Mr Blair told parliament that Iraq could unleash chemical weapons within forty-five minutes. He did not make clear that this alleged capability applied only to short-range battlefield weapons, and the statement was widely misinterpreted to apply to long range weapons that put, for example, Cyprus within range. The misunderstanding was evident in an *Evening Standard* headline – '45 Minutes from Attack' – on the evening of Mr Blair's speech. Number 10 did not, however, rush to clear up this misunderstanding. It was favourable to their cause.

Using language designed to create favourable misunderstandings displays the same lack of intellectual integrity. It shows a willingness to trick people into agreeing with your policies. It is not what we should expect from a 'pretty straight sort of guy'.[11] Though perhaps we should expect it from someone who keeps telling us how straight he is.

5 Beautifully Said!

Plato disapproved of the way poets express themselves. They stir up emotions with beautiful language. That would be fine if plays and poems were simply pleasing sights and sounds, like fireworks displays and instrumental music. But they are not. They insinuate ideas, which the audience is inclined to believe simply because it gets caught up in the emotion. Poets are enemies of reason. Plato thought they should be banished from the ideal republic.

Given its decline in popularity, poetry no longer threatens the rational fabric of society. Plato would probably allow poets to live anonymously amongst us in their bedsits and derelict caravans.

Gospel music. That's what Plato would want banned nowadays. Those gospel tunes are catchy. They make you want to tap your toe and sing along, or even wave your hands in the air and weep. That's their point. As every guru knows, get people chanting your chant and you will soon have them walking your walk and cashing your cheques.

Plato would probably object not only to Gospel music but

to the whole pop-music industry. 'Get up, get on up, stay on the scene, like a sex machine': that's good clean fun. But few pop musicians can stick to the straight and narrow path followed by James Brown. They discover human rights or environmentalism or something else important and we are no longer invited to shake our money-makers but to free-ee Nelson Mandela, to feed the world or to use recyclable paper. It is strangely difficult to sing along without agreeing and, when the tune is good, difficult not to sing along.

I doubt Plato would like modern politicians much either. They play the same lyrical game. They substitute compelling language for proper reasoning. 'Substitute' is the important word here. There is nothing wrong with a memorable slogan when it encapsulates a politician's serious ideas: when the slogan is not all he has to offer. Metaphors, too, are fine provided their literal meaning is clear. Then they add beauty to a politician's expression with no loss of rigour.

Unfortunately, politicians rarely stick to these rules. Their rhetoric is full of empty slogans and metaphors whose literal meaning is opaque. They attempt to win our support not by reasoned argument but by expressing themselves nicely: by the rhetorical equivalent of putting their ideas to a catchy tune.

*

The best known slogan of recent political history is probably Labour's 'Tough on crime, tough on the causes of crime'. I have often heard it recited in a mocking tone, as if it were the kind of empty slogan to which we should object.

This is unfair. 'Tough on crime, tough on the causes of crime' is a model slogan. It encapsulates a clear idea: that the government will deter those who have already developed a criminal disposition while simultaneously trying to prevent people from developing such a disposition in the first place.

And real policies lie behind the slogan. Our civil liberties have been curtailed to make it easier to convict those accused of crimes and changes to sentencing laws mean that Britain's prison population has increased significantly during Labour's term in office. The causes of crime have also been addressed, at least if you agree with the Labour Party that crime is caused by income inequality, or 'poverty' as Mr Blair would call it. The Labour government has increased income and property tax on the rich, introduced a minimum wage and increased means tested benefits.

You may disapprove of these policies but that is beside the present point. Labour is doing what you might expect from a party that is tough on crime and tough on the causes of crime. Few political slogans, however, share the virtues of TOCTOTCOC. Most are wholly independent creatures, supported by no serious ideas or actual policies. They are merely words.

My earliest memory of a political slogan comes from the 1975 general election in New Zealand. The leader of the National Party, Robert Muldoon, promised the electorate 'New Zealand the way you want it'. He did not, however, make it clear who he meant by 'you'. Insofar as he was talking to every voter, some were sure to be disappointed, because not everybody wanted New Zealand the same way. The slogan managed to combine emptiness with certain falsity, which is quite an achievement. Nevertheless, it was considered a master stroke and given much of the credit for Mr Muldoon's victory.

Things are not much better thirty years later on the other side of the world. The virtuous TOTTOTCOC is the exception rather than the rule when it comes to Mr Blair's slogans. Consider one of his favourites:

No rights without responsibilities.

Mr Blair rarely uses this slogan in conjunction with a verb. But he cannot be claiming that there *are*, in fact, no rights without responsibilities. For, although this is true, it isn't true in the sense that Mr Blair means it. If you have a right then everybody else has a duty or responsibility to respect that right. Your right to life, for example, imposes on everybody else a duty not to kill you. But Mr Blair makes it clear that he is talking about rights and responsibilities for the same person. It is more like 'no pudding without eating your meat'.

In which case, Mr Blair's slogan cannot be reporting a fact but must be making a suggestion. Because, as things stand, we certainly do have rights that burden us with no responsibilities. Your right to life creates no responsibilities for you. It is other people's right to life that does that. Or consider the presence of your name in someone's will. That gives you a responsibility-free entitlement.

No rights without responsibilities sounds like a radical suggestion. What radical new policies will embody this principle? The slogan is usually heard when Mr Blair is discussing people who engage in what he calls anti-social behaviour: neighbours who play loud music at night, raise unkempt and foul-mouthed children, let their dogs shit in public stairwells and that sort of thing. Such people often receive assistance from the government and Mr Blair suggests that it ought to be cut off if they do not stop their irresponsible behaviour. This is the kind of thing Mr Blair is proposing under his slogan.

It is a small policy for such a big slogan. It involves no more than a small extension of the laws that prevent people from being a nuisance, and a new penalty for the crime: namely, the loss of welfare benefits. There is no radical new principle at work here. All crimes consist in failing to do what you have a duty to do: i.e. in falling short of your responsibilities. And crimes have always been punished by the loss of what you normally have a right to, such as your money or liberty. Mr Blair recites his slogan as if it were a big new idea. But the idea of punishing crimes is not really new, and the crimes and punishments Mr Blair has in mind are not really big. It is an empty slogan.

*

Slogans are easy to spot and the population has developed a degree of scepticism about them. Metaphorical language, however, attracts much less sceptical attention, perhaps because political rhetoric is so thoroughly metaphorical that people have become desensitised. Politicians rarely describe or justify their policies plainly in literal language. They prefer to give us the gist with metaphors.

Mr Blair explains his public services policies, for example, in terms of clothes-making. He has rejected a 'one-size-fits-all' approach in favour of services that are 'tailored to the individual'. Then, shifting from Savile Row to the M1, he informs us that consumers of health and education will 'drive' the service. Where to, he does not tell us, but such well-dressed drivers will surely head towards the leading edge.

Such language gives the listener the impression of understanding. The sentences are grammatically correct and these are familiar metaphors. But it is only an impression. For the purpose of assessing Mr Blair's proposals such language is wholly inadequate. It does not tell us what he really proposes to do. Consider the following description of his choice-based public services policy:

> We are proposing to put an entirely different dynamic in place to drive our public services: one where the service will be driven not by the government or by the managers but by the user – the patient, the parent, the pupil and the law abiding citizen.[12]

What, in literal terms, is all this driving? How will patients drive the NHS or law abiding citizens drive the criminal justice system? The speech from which this statement is taken does not even attempt to answer this question. Yet it is a speech in which Mr Blair claims to explain his new public services policy.

Nor does Mr Blair have anything literal to say about the benefits of the policy. Perhaps he is suckered by his own metaphors. What need is there to justify policies that replace our ill-fitting off-the-rack clothes with snug tailor made outfits, or that increase our chance of going where we want by placing our hands on the steering wheel? Alas, we are not really talking about clothes or car journeys. We are talking about health and education policies. Why are Mr Blair's specific proposals a good idea? All this metaphorical waffle cannot answer that question.

Discussion of Britain's EU policies is even more polluted with inscrutable metaphor. In May 2004, for example, the Foreign Secretary, Jack Straw, defended his desire to sign Britain up to the new European constitutional treaty:

> Britain, as a successful nation state and major player
> on the world stage, has a strategic interest in being at
> the heart of Europe. Our prosperity and security de-
> pend on it.[13]

Mr Straw did not explain why Britain's prosperity and security depend on being at the heart of Europe. The fact that Britain is a major player on the world stage, the Sir Lawrence Olivier of nations, seems irrelevant. If anything, alliances are less important to big powerful nations, like the US, than they are to small weak ones, like Ireland or Portugal.

Yet the main problem with Mr Straw's position – the reason he must have found it difficult to mount an argument in its favour – is the difficulty in telling what it is. What does it mean to be at the heart of Europe? Where must a country go to be there? If I do not know where the metaphorical heart of Europe is, I cannot know whether Mr Straw is right that locating Britain anywhere else will make us poor and insecure.

Tom Utley explained the problem in his *Daily Telegraph* column:

> When the Europhiles are not telling us that we must be at the heart of Europe, they are saying that we will miss the boat, or the bus, if we don't agree to the constitution. Either that, or we will lose our place at the top table. Language matters, and this sort of language just won't do. There are a great many Britons who are genuinely anxious to hear the arguments for accepting the new constitution. None of this talk of hearts, boats, top tables and players on world stages throws any light on the matter.[14]

Of course, politicians use such language precisely to avoid throwing light on the matter. As the prostitutes of Amsterdam's red light district age, so they sit further back from the window and dim the lights. Their old bodies don't bear close inspection under bright lights. The same goes for many political policies. The clear light of plain language would make their wrinkles all too evident. Better to present them veiled behind opaque metaphors.

6 Hooray!

What is the difference between justice and pumpkin? There are many, of course, but I have a particular difference in mind. Whereas everyone agrees what pumpkin is without necessarily liking it, everyone likes justice without necessarily agreeing what it is. 'Pumpkin' is a plain, descriptive word. It simply refers to a kind of vegetable. 'Justice' is a hooray word. What it means is not perfectly clear but, whatever someone takes it to mean, he will think it's a good thing.

That is why a politician need neither hesitate nor think before declaring that he seeks more justice in Britain. No one will know exactly what he means, but everyone will approve of the plan. He can win support without having to commit himself to anything he might regret later. If he promises more pumpkin, on the other hand, everyone will know what he means. Some will disagree with the plan and everyone will know if it fails.

'Justice' isn't the only hooray word. There is also 'modern', 'progress', 'fair', and 'equality', amongst others. Politicians use such words relentlessly but they will never tell you precisely what they mean by them. Usually this is because they do not know what they mean by them. But even those who do gain nothing by spelling it out. That would only spoil these words' magical power to win agreement.

The 2001 Labour Party manifesto states:

> We are a broad-based movement for progress and social justice.

Who can say what this means? What policies would such a party favour? How does this make Labour differ from its political rivals? No one can know. Nor, however, will anyone disapprove. No one wants a narrow-based movement for regression and anti-social injustice. Substituting for 'progress' and 'social justice' plainly descriptive words, such as 'gay rights' and 'redistribution of wealth', would have aided clarity, but not popularity. Many people do not care for gay rights or the redistribution of wealth.

Using unexplained hooray words keeps a politician on safe ground but at the cost of rendering his declarations empty. Of course he favours justice, fairness and the British way. Every British politician does. What we voters need to know is what he means by all these things, what he thinks they amount to, where his view of them differs from his rivals'. Alas, we never get this information. We only get the platitudes.

*

Mr Blair is keen on fairness. He rarely passes up an opportunity to recommend it to us or to claim that his policies promote it. But what does he mean by it?

Before getting to what Mr Blair means, it is worth noting a broad disagreement about fairness. There are those who think it concerns the distribution of goods, and those who think it concerns procedures. Roughly, Distributionists think a situation is fair if goods are allocated evenly across members of society. Proceduralists think a situation is fair if it is arrived at via a fair process. According to Proceduralists, you cannot tell whether a situation is fair simply by looking at the distribution of goods. An unequal distribution can be fair provided it was arrived at via a fair process, as when someone wins the grand prize in a lottery. And an equal distribution is unfair when achieved via an unfair process, as when someone steals the lucky man's lottery winnings and distributes them amongst all the losers.

That is putting the matter simply. You can, of course, hold complex views of fairness that include Distributionist and Proceduralist elements. But if you aim to make your views on fairness clear, you will have to explain where you stand on this issue because these two views give diametrically opposed answers to questions about what is fair.

Are means-tested pensions fair, for example? A Distributionist will say yes; they help to smooth the distribution of goods across society. A Proceduralist will say no; if one man worked hard and saved while another was lazy and wasteful, it is only fair that the former should be wealthier than the latter in his retirement. It is no good a politician's saying simply that he favours a fair pensions system. If we do not know where he stands on the Distributionism versus Proceduralism issue, we won't know what policies to expect from him, nor whether we really agree with him when he tells us that he wants the system to be fair.

Where, then, does Mr Blair stand? As a member of Labour Party, you might expect him to favour Distributionism. That has traditionally been the view of Socialists. And, indeed, he often says things that suggest it. During his speech to the 2004 Labour Party Conference, for example, this was the last of his ten pledges:

A fair deal for all at work. An opportunity society is one in which we stop ignoring the lives of the millions of hard working low paid families who do the jobs that we all rely on ... For them, we offer not just the respect they deserve, but the guarantee of a decent income, a rising minimum wage, equal pay between men and women, four weeks paid holidays from now on plus bank holidays.[15]

Fairness is here associated with levelling the distribution of incomes, between high paid and low paid and between men and women. And Mr Blair often associates fairness with making things available to 'the many, not the few'. He often sounds like a traditional Socialist Distributionist.

On other occasions, however, Mr Blair seems to promote a Proceduralist view. In May 1997, for example, he declared:

In Britain today there are now up to 150,000 people earning more than £100,000 a year. Success hard-earned and reward fairly-gained are essential to a successful society, and I for one salute the hard work and enterprise that has helped some people achieve wealth for themselves and their families.[16]

More generally, Mr Blair claims to believe in meritocracy: the idea that people are entitled to what they obtain by merit. Add to this the fact that merit is unequally distributed, and you have the opposite of a Distributionist ideology.

Perhaps Mr Blair has one of those subtle views of fairness I mentioned earlier that combines Distributionist and Proceduralist elements. He doesn't explain it to us only because it is so subtle that he fears we could not understand it. Or perhaps he simply uses the word 'fair' to describe any policy he favours. When the policy redistributes wealth we get the impression he is a Distributionist; when it tolerates in-equality on meritocratic grounds, we think he is a Proceduralist.

In either case, we are lost. We cannot predict which poli-cies Mr Blair will consider fair. And we cannot tell if fairness, as understood by Mr Blair, is something that we should seek in a policy. Which means that Mr Blair's avowed devotion to fairness should be of no interest to us.

*

Hooray words, as used by politicians, have no meaning. Or, at least, no meaning clear enough to convey any information. But they do have a flavour. Strictly, the Conservatives could describe themselves as a broad-based movement for progress and social justice, but you know they won't. These words do not suit them. They are not good Tory words. Tories prefer words like 'hard work', 'family' and 'common sense'. When leader of the Conservative Party, William Hague even prom-ised a 'common sense revolution'. God knows what one of those would look like but it must be better than a slow creep of uncommon stupidity.

Political positioning is not so much a matter of policies as of preferred words. The Labour and Conservative parties have very similar policies. They recommend similar levels of tax-ation and government spending. Both favour identity cards as a way of preventing benefit fraud, terrorism and illegal immi-gration. Both want to extend choice to the users of public services without privatising them. In Labour's hands these policies are all about progress, equality and social justice. In Conservative hands, they are common sense ways of crack-ing down on criminals and encouraging hard work.

Mr Blair's 1997 election victory brought with it a whole new political philosophy: the Third Way. You might expect a whole new political philosophy to have dramatic effects on policy. We were in line for some serious reforms. People were going to think unthinkable things and we would soon live at the 'radical centre'. Brace yourself!

Yet, at the same time, Mr Blair let us know that he wasn't going to do anything too dramatic. He was not a boat rocker or golden goose killer. He promised not to increase income tax and to stick to the Conservatives' budget for two years. And he has been pretty good to this part of his word. If you considered only the policies implemented since 1997 it would be hard to tell that John Major's Conservative government had lost power.

John Major had the Private Finance Initiative, Citizens Charter and league tables for schools. He massively expanded the numbers attending university. He was broadly pro-European but hesitant about joining the single currency. Only reforming the House of Lords and establishing political assemblies in Wales and Scotland has marked any significant departure from John Major's agenda, and these changes have no special connection with the Third Way.

Mr Blair's new political philosophy did not bring new policies with it, only new words. Mr Major wanted us to get back to basics; Mr Blair wants us to recognise that there are no rights without responsibilities. Mr Major offered us a class-less society; Mr Blair offers an opportunity society.

The superiority of the Third Way lies not in its policy implications but in expanding the range of words available to the Labour Party. They still have all their old words: 'equality', 'social justice' and so on. These get used at Labour Party conferences. But Mr Blair has also appropriated Conservative words, such as 'enterprise' and 'responsibility'. He can hardly go ten minutes these days without mentioning 'hard working families'.

By taking command of the whole range of hooray words, Mr Blair has put the Conservatives in a difficult position.

They no longer have any linguistic space of their own. To distinguish themselves from the government, they may even be forced to adopt some significantly different policies.

PART III
Quick and Easy

My mother often defends an opinion by pointing out that it is shared by my aunt or by one of her friends. These opinions sometimes concern weighty matters: good investments, politics, who should coach the All Blacks and so on.

My aunt and my mother's friends are reasonable people but they are not experts on very much. The simple fact that they believe something is not a good reason to agree. If my mother wants to convince me that I should invest all my money in pork belly futures, for example, then she will have to provide a proper justification for doing so. She will have to show, to a reasonable degree of confidence, that the return from this investment will exceed the opportunity cost: that no other use of the money is likely to yield a higher return.

Giving such a justification is difficult. You can see why my mother prefers simply to point to the opinion's popularity with her friends. Defending political policies is also difficult. You need to show not only what the effects of the policy are likely to be but also why we should favour these effects. A proper justification cannot help but drag you into economics and political philosophy, which are difficult subjects. You can see why politicians try to justify their policies in other ways.

Three alternative justifications are especially popular. Like my mother, politicians will appeal to the opinions of non-experts, advertising their policy on the ground that most people support it. Or they will tell us that their policy is better than the alternative offered by their main political rival, as though there were no other options. Or they will claim that there are in fact no alternatives to their policy: that while the political system may provide us with two or three options, reality provides us with only one.

Voters may also prefer these quick and easy arguments. A proper policy justification is difficult not only to develop but also to follow and assess. It asks a lot of both author and audience, and few enjoy hard intellectual work. Most will prefer the user-friendly alternatives offered by politicians. But that is irrelevant. An argument's validity is not guaranteed by its popularity. There is no democratic substitute for logic.

7 By Command of the People

Management consultants suffer a systematic temptation towards corruption, summed up perfectly in a conversation I once had with a director at my old firm. He had explained the advice he favoured giving our client. It did not strike me as very good advice.

> 'Is that what you really believe?' I asked.
> 'I don't care what I believe,' he replied, 'I care what the client believes.'

The short-term interests of a management consultant can be served by telling clients not what is true but what they want to hear. That is what will win you the follow-on project. And if the advice is bad, well, that will be hard to tell, since these things take time and in business there are always many factors that explain failure. You'll probably get away with it.

Politicians face the same temptation. Like management consultants, politicians need their ideas to be not just right but popular. Indeed, provided they are popular, it doesn't matter too much if they are right. As with business strategies, it takes a while to see that policies have gone wrong and you may well be able to evade taking the blame in any event.

But the temptation gets politicians much more muddled than consultants. No consultant would defend a strategy by saying to his client: 'This is the strategy you want me to advise you to follow: the one that will get me rehired.' That may be a good reason for the consultant to advise the strategy, but it is not a good reason for the client to follow it. Yet politicians commit this absurd error all the time. They recommend their policies on the ground that they are the policies that people support – not just privately to their colleagues when planning election strategy, but when explaining the merits of their policies to the public.

Mr Blair, for example, recently explained why it is a good idea to increase the number of policemen patrolling neighbourhoods:

> First, we seek to revive community policing. People
> want not just the bobby on the beat, but a strong, or-
> ganised uniformed presence back on the streets. And
> the local community itself wants a say in how they
> are policed. They want to be in charge. Our proposals
> for police, CSOs and neighbourhood action do that.[17]

Perhaps a return to community policing is a good idea, but not because the people support it. Hopefully, it is the other way around; they support it because it is a good idea, because it is the best way of reducing crime. Properly to defend the policy Mr Blair needs to explain why it really is the best way of reducing crime. Which he fails to do by simply pointing out that many people think it is.

Despite its vacuity, no defence of policies is more popular with politicians. We are endlessly told which policies are supported by 'the people of this nation' or by the now fashionable 'hard working families'. It may be empty, but the argument has a deliciously democratic ring to it. Who could deny that the policies supported by the majority are those that should be implemented? Are you an enemy of the people?

Democracy may deserve its sacred status, but this argument confuses procedural with substantive issues. Consider trial by jury. The jury decides the question of guilt. But that does not mean that the prosecuting barrister could establish guilt by pointing out that, at the beginning of the trial, the jury was disposed to think the accused guilty. He must mount a case for guilt using evidence about the presence of the accused at the crime scene, his motives for committing the crime and so on. The opinions of the jury are no part of the case whatsoever. It is the other way around; their opinions ought to be formed by the cases made by the barristers.

Democracy is the same. In a democracy, the people – that is, the majority of people or the largest minority – choose the government and, where referenda are involved, they directly choose policies. But it does not follow from this that what makes a policy the best available is that it is supported by the majority. The majority is perfectly capable of supporting the wrong policy. If you are a democrat, you will think they should get their way, but you need not think that the way they get is best. Democrats needn't believe in the infallibility of the people.

It should go without saying amongst democrats that the policies chosen by the people will get implemented, or at least that the party elected will take power. What doesn't go without saying, and what politicians need to convince voters of, is which policies are best. And that cannot be settled by opinion polls. Those who argue as if it can – who claim that an idea must be correct because the majority thinks it is – commit the so-called *democratic fallacy*.

*

The democratic fallacy is popular with politicians because agreeing with the majority is helpful when it comes to getting elected, and because this self-serving intellectual laziness can be passed off as a democratic virtue.

Elitism, on the other hand, is not well thought of these days, especially in the Labour Party. So we less often encounter the *elitist fallacy*. You do not hear the argument that some idea must be true because everyone with an income over £100,000 a year agrees with it, or because it is fashionable at the Garrick club. But some special kinds of elitism are fine in the Labour Party and they can be used to provide instant justifications for contentious ideas.

In June 2004 Mr Blair explained why his policy of increasing consumer choice in education and healthcare was a good idea:

> I believe the vast majority of those on the centre-left now believe in the new personalised concept of public services.[18]

The vast majority on the centre-left may be very clever people. But has their reliability been so well established that their agreement confirms an idea? Is disagreeing with the majority on the centre-left really a recipe for error?

The argument doesn't just set you to wondering about the infallibility of the centre-left. It also makes you wonder how Mr Blair knows what they believe. Did he conduct a survey? How did he know whom to count and whom to exclude? 'Centre-left' is a vague term. He obviously does not take his own opinions to define the centre-left, since then it would be everyone on the centre-left and not just a vast majority who believe in 'the new personalised concept of public services'.

Mr Blair enjoys a mysterious power to know the mind of

the people. In December 2004 he gave a democratic explanation of why his Third Way policies are best:

> People don't want a minimalist state, but nor do they want the old centralised state. Instead, they want the state to empower them, to give them the means to make the most of their own lives.[19]

How did he know that this is what people want? It is an extraordinary insight on his part. The notions involved – minimalist state, centralised state and empowering state – are so ill-defined that even the results of an opinion poll would be difficult to interpret. And, as far as I know, he has no such opinion poll results at his disposal.

Mr Blair is to the people what the Pope is to God. He knows what the people want by some special power of democratic intuition. Fortunately for him, they always seem to want his policies.

*

Some politicians practice an interesting variation on the democratic fallacy. They argue that something must be made compulsory because people want to do it.

During the 1997 election campaign, for example, I heard Alex Salmond, leader of Scottish Nationalist Party, criticise New Labour for promising not to increase income tax. He explained that the people of Scotland wanted more spent on the education of their children and were willing to have their income tax increased to fund it. That is to say, they wanted to do what Mr Salmond's policy would make them do.

But if people really did want to spend more of their income on education, they were free to do so. They could hire private tutors for their children or donate money to local schools to improve facilities or hire extra teachers. The only justification for increasing tax to spend on something is that the money would not otherwise be spent on it. Mr Salmond wanted to increase income tax and spending on education precisely because he doubted people would spend the money if not compelled to. A policy of compulsion may be right, but it cannot be right because people want to do what they will now be compelled to do.

It isn't only some on the Left who claim that people should be compelled to do what they prefer to do. John Hayes, Conservative MP for South Holland and Deeping, recently wrote an article in *The Spectator* lamenting a new liberalism infecting the Conservative Party.[20] He claimed that the party should adopt a policy of actively promoting certain virtues, such as 'duty, restraint and loyalty'. Why? Because these are the values of the vast majority of British citizens. Yet if they are, why would the government need to promote them? Why waste money encouraging the values that people already have?

Mr Hayes favours policies that promote his values. You would expect him to justify this idea on the ground that his values are right but sadly uncommon. Alas, that would look undemocratic. Who is he to impose his values on a population that does not share them? So instead he claims that his values should be imposed on people precisely because they share them. It may be crazy but at least it's democratic.

8 Resistance Is Futile

There are two things you shouldn't resist: the good and the inevitable. Resisting the former makes the world a worse place. Resisting the latter is a guaranteed waste of time and effort.

This means that when seeking acquiescence, you must usually convince people of the merits of your proposal. For very little is inevitable. Death and taxes, perhaps, but not much else. And even then, neither the rate of tax nor the precise time of death are certain.

Demonstrating the merits of your proposals, however, is often difficult. And even when you succeed, people can be infuriatingly reluctant to see reason. So it is sometimes tempting to claim that your good ideas are also inevitable, even when they are not. I have heard men telling women who were clearly not attracted to them that their eventual sexual congress was inevitable anyway. Why the futile resistance? Go with the flow!

Political seducers are no different. They will often tell you that what they propose is unavoidable. There is no point resisting their agenda, no point considering its pros and cons, when it is sure to come about anyway.

It is an absurd argument insofar as it is intended to win your vote. If something really is inevitable, then it should make no difference to how you cast your vote; it will happen whoever comes to power. But the absurdity of an argument never stopped a politician making it.

*

The simplest and most popular way of claiming that a policy is inevitable is to say that there is no alternative. Margaret Thatcher famously claimed that there was no alternative to her economic policies. The statement was obviously false. If what you suggest is a change, then there must be at least one alternative: namely, the status quo. And there will usually be many other options as well: all the other possible changes that you haven't suggested.

You might charitably interpret the statement 'there is no alternative' as an ellipsis in which the word 'better' has been omitted. What Mrs Thatcher meant to say was that there was no better alternative. But that would be too charitable. If that were what she meant, it would not have been a statement that ended debate but one that began it. Mrs Thatcher would have had to show that her policies really were the best available. Yet avoiding any such debate is precisely what the claim that there is no alternative is supposed to achieve. If there is only one choice, it must be the best choice.

Mr Blair used to cast himself as Mrs Thatcher's natural successor and, in this respect at least, he seems to be right. He often claims that his policies are the only option.

In January 2000, for example, Mr Blair announced his plan to increase state funding for healthcare while simultaneously creating so-called Foundation Hospitals and giving the private sector a greater role in providing state funded healthcare.

He knew that many on the left of his party would object. They can be relied upon to welcome any increase in government spending but they are not nearly so keen on Public-Private Partnerships (PPPs), to which they have some serious objections. PPPs do not really transfer financial risk away from the state, they make accountability unclear, they are a more expensive source of funds than government debt and, because PPP contracts typically grant private firms effective monopolies, there is no competitive pressure for them to be cost efficient. Such objections sound serious but, like any other objections, they may be set aside if there is no alternative to Mr Blair's policy. Which is precisely what he claimed.[21]

There are, of course, many alternatives to Mr Blair's favoured policy for health care in Britain: every other country in Europe presents one, as does the United States, New Zealand and Australia. But he did not let that deter him from claiming that there are none. There is something mesmerising about obvious falsehoods declared with conviction.

He did it again in January 2004 during the debate about university top up fees. Top up fees allow universities to charge students higher tuition fees: up to £3,000 a year for the best universities. Top-up fees are one way of addressing the problem of universities' under-funding. Mr Blair claimed that they are the only way. Or, more precisely, he claimed that 'there is no plan B'.[22] But there are many other options: plans B right through to Z and beyond. I'll suggest two here. Increase income tax and spend the money on universities. Or privatise the universities and allow them to charge whatever fees they like. Mr Blair's task was to show that his policy was better than these and other alternatives. Instead he claimed that no such alternatives even exist.

*

The 'no alternative' ploy has a shortcoming. Alternatives are usually quite apparent. Claiming that they do not exist can draw unwanted attention to them. So it is often better to suggest the inevitability of your policies in a more subtle way.

Mr Blair favours grand historical narrative. He tells the story of political progress in a way that makes his policies the natural next step. His stories have the *thesis-antithesis-synthesis* structure that the 'dialectical' philosophers, George Hegel, Karl Marx and Mao Tse Tung, claimed all human history must follow. Mr Blair's policies, like those of Hegel, Marx and Mao before him, are, of course, the synthesis. Here is an example:

> The world has changed, and continues to change dramatically, and so we cannot respond in the old ways to social and economic challenges. In the 1950s and 1960s the big question in politics was: what can the state achieve? In the 1970s and 1980s it was: what can the individual achieve? Neither of these are right for the new century. Today the question we must answer is: what can society achieve – not the state on its own, not individuals on their own, but all of us together as a community, where opportunity for all is matched by responsibility from all?[23]

Mr Blair's 'Third Way' between the extremes of Statism and Individualism is the necessary next step in history, forced upon us by the dramatic changes taking place in the world. To vote against it is to fight the tide of progress.

Mr Blair's history in the above quotation is dubious. It exaggerates the differences between his recommended policies and what preceded them. In Thatcher's 1980s, which Mr Blair says were all about the individual, the state continued to play a significant role in Britain. Aggregate taxation remained high, at about 40% of GDP, funding universal healthcare, education and pensions as well as unemployment benefits and state housing. It was a mixed, private and public system of precisely the kind that Mr Blair advocates.

But even if Mr Blair's facts were not wonky, his logic still would be. How does it follow from the fact that the world is changing, or from Mr Blair's potted political history, that his Third Way is the best policy agenda? Mr Blair makes no case for his claim that 'today the question we must answer is: what can society achieve – not the state on its own, not individuals on their own, but all of us together as a community, where opportunity for all is matched by responsibility from all'. He simply says it is, hoping you will be seduced by his story in which his Third Way is a synthesis of the Statism and Individualism that came before. But why isn't a return to Statism just what we need? Or more Individualism? Telling the story of what went before cannot answer the question of what should come next.

Another, closely related ploy for making policies appear inevitable is claiming that they are not policies at all but externally imposed conditions to which we must respond. The great changes taking place are described, if at all, as though they were events beyond the control of any politician. Some really are, such as natural disasters or technological developments. But most are not.

Globalisation is a favourite external force for Mr Blair and most other modern politicians. His policies are frequently cast as responses to it.[24] But insofar as globalisation refers to free cross-border trade, investment and migration, it is the product of political decisions. Restrictive trade policies made the world less globalised in the 1950s than it had been in the 1890s. And even in today's relatively global economy, all regimes choose to opt out to a lesser or greater extent. North Koreans live in near complete isolation from the rest of the world and even the US continues to impose trade and immigration restrictions. Those who resist globalisation may be making a mistake, but not the mistake of fighting the inevitable.

When discussing some tawdry political manoeuvring in Britain, a *Daily Telegraph* editorial declared that 'there is no point in whining about any of these things; they are the facts of modern political life'.[25] This is the sentiment of worldly-wise realism that politicians hope to exploit when they tell you how things are. They hope you will slip quietly from thinking that this is how things are to the very different idea that this is how things should be – or, at least, that resistance is futile.

This *Daily Telegraph* reasoning, that it is pointless to complain about a fact, is nonsense. Should we complain about things that are not facts? That would be truly pointless. Perhaps we should complain about nothing at all. Some monks might agree but it is hard to believe from a newspaper editorialist.

The 'facts of modern political life' are not like the more general 'facts of life'. They are not something that cannot be changed and that we might as well get used to. Political facts change all the time, and not only in the direction preordained by Mr Blair and those others who claim to know the inexorable path of history. How they change depends on the actions taken by politicians. That is why they need to convince us that the changes they intend to make are the right ones. Which they do not achieve by pretending that they will happen anyway.

9 Just the Two of Us

Creationists believe the biblical story of the Earth's origin. They believe, among other things, that the world was created around 4000BC by a word. The word was God and the word was with God.[26] (God was apparently beside himself at the time of creation, which is understandable.)

This theory has at least two problems. It is inconsistent with what modern scientists believe about the age of the Earth, which they estimate to be not 6000 but 4.5 billion years old. And there is no evidence for the theory, beyond the opinions of the authors of relevant bits of the Bible, who we cannot regard as reliable sources: they fail to explain either their evidence or their research methods.

Creationists are acutely aware of the first problem. They devote much energy to challenging contemporary theories about the age of the Earth and its natural history: evolution, dinosaurs and all that nonsense. But they fail to notice the second problem. They argue as though refuting the contemporary scientific view would suffice to establish the truth of

Creationism. They argue as if modern science and Creationism were the only options.

They are not. There are also the creation stories of the world's other pre-enlightenment cultures. Establishing the truth of Creationism by a process of elimination would require the refutation of these stories too. And not just these stories but all those possible creation stories that have not been made up but could have been – that the earth is a giant pomegranate that fell off the back of a cosmic fruit truck or was created three weeks ago by the number 12 or whatever you like.

When there are infinitely many possible answers, you cannot gain victory for your hypothesis by eliminating the alternatives: there will always be another you have not yet defeated. And you certainly cannot win by eliminating just one of them. Creationists who think that they can prove their position by attacking the popular scientific view commit the *false dichotomy* fallacy. They argue as though there were only two possibilities when in fact there are many.

*

What's good for the priest is good for the politician. Here is Mr Blair explaining the merit of his policy to extend consumer choice in the public services:

> This is a vision which combines choice, excellence and equality in a modern universal welfare state. We will contrast such a vision with that of the Conservatives whose essential anti-public service ideology is shown by their policy to subsidise a few to opt-out of public services at the expense of the many; to abandon targets for public service performance; and to cut the overall amount of public spending drastically.[27]

Why will Mr Blair contrast his policy with the Conservatives'? Perhaps his policy really is better than theirs, but that is irrelevant. There are many more than these two options. Mr Blair is committing the false dichotomy fallacy.

Some may think I am failing to take account of Britain's first-past-the-post electoral system, which means that elections are usually a 'two horse race'. In a two horse race, all that matters is which is faster, not whether either is very fast. In a two party system, the dichotomy is real, not false.

Sometimes this is a fair point. In the weeks leading up to polling day, for example, negative campaigning is perfectly legitimate. To win our votes, a politician need only convince us that what he offers is better than our other options. We should prefer a mediocre candidate if he can show his opponents to be terrible. But this is rarely the context in which attacks on the opposition take place.

In the speech quoted above, Mr Blair was not explaining why people should vote Labour at the next general election. The next election was then about a year away. He was explaining his public services policy to an audience at Guy's and St Thomas' hospital in London. He needed to show why his policy is the best way of improving Britain's public services. When that was the issue, the quality of the Conservatives' policy is beside the point.

In fact, his attack on the Conservatives only makes his argument worse. If their policy really is hopeless, then having a better one is no great achievement. A policy could improve on the Conservatives' and yet still be quite bad. Mr Blair would do better to praise the Conservatives: to say that although his policy is better, theirs is very good. Who is it more impressive to beat over 100 metres: Carl Lewis or Luciano Pavarotti?

Rarely is a politician arguing directly for our votes. More

often he is trying to justify his policies. Why did he pick this one ahead of all his other options. British voters may have only three serious options when voting, but politicians have countlessly many when choosing their policies. They cannot show that they have made the best choice by showing that it is better than the two options chosen by their rivals.

*

When the question is simply who voters should prefer, as it is every few years, it is fair enough to promote yourself by discrediting your opposition. Yet, even then, politicians usually fail to make their case properly, because they commit the *straw man* fallacy. They set up an absurd caricature of their opponents' ideas so that they may knock it down more easily.

This is how Mr Blair summed up the choice facing the electorate in 1997:

> That is the difference between the parties. [The Conservatives] say Britain cannot be better. We say it can and must be better. The difference is as old as politics itself: progress versus stagnation, the courage to change versus the fear of the unknown, the belief that we are stronger together than we are alone.

I followed the 1997 election campaign closely. I do not remember John Major or any other Conservative saying that Britain could not get better. Perhaps Mr Blair caught something that I missed, but it seems unlikely. I have never heard a politician running for election who claimed that he could not make things better. Mr Blair would have us believe that the Conservatives are very odd people.

Not only odd but evil. Who but a villain would favour stagnation over progress, promote fear over courage, and hold the view that everyone is better off alone? It sends a shudder up your spine to think of such people. Or it would, if you could believe this hysterical nonsense.

During the same campaign, the Conservatives ran the notorious 'demon eyes' poster campaign. It showed the smiling mask ripped away from Mr Blair's face to reveal the red-eyed demon beneath. Voters are used to politicians demonizing each other, but only metaphorically. Going literal was probably a step too far. The campaign was considered a tactical blunder.

Such absurd misrepresentation of your rivals is also a logical blunder. Of course we would prefer Mr Major to the man depicted in the 'demon eyes' posters, and prefer Mr Blair to someone who says that Britain cannot improve. But since neither of these reprehensible characters exist, the argument is worthless. You cannot show your opponent wrong by refuting an opinion he does not really hold, nor show yourself the better man by pointing to flaws he does not really possess.

*

Britain's first-past-the-post electoral system encourages the false dichotomy and straw man fallacies. The fact that there are usually only two parties seriously competing for government can make the criticism of rivals seem relevant when it is not, and tempts politicians to exaggerate their opponents' shortcomings. It also means, however, that there is usually little to choose between the parties. The way modern political parties formulate policies makes it likely that they will arrive at the same answers.

Each party has its dependable voters. They may be ignored when it comes to policy formulation, since they will vote for you in any event. Then there are those who will definitely vote for the other party. They too may be ignored. It is only voters who might be swung either way who really matter. Political policy advisers try to determine which policies will appeal to these swing voters, or at least to as many of them as possible. Insofar as parties have competent advisers, they will offer the same policies.

Sometimes significant policy differences emerge. In the 1983 and 1987 general elections, British voters faced a stark choice. The Conservative and Labour parties were then led by people with genuine political ideologies, and the marketing techniques which now guide the formulation of policy were in their infancy. Since 1992, however, it has been hard to distinguish the policies of the two main parties.

The Conservatives' policies on health and education, for example, are so similar to Mr Blair's that only a 'policy wonk' could tell them apart. The Conservatives also want to increase consumer choice in the public services without privatising them or introducing prices. If Mr Blair believes his policy is right then he must think the Conservatives' policy is roughly right too. They may genuinely disagree when it comes to the details of their choice-based public services policies but that is mere quibbling. They should drop the absurd pretence that the sky will fall in if their rival's policies are adopted.

The same goes for the other choices with which the two main parties present us. They are rarely as dramatic as the parties claim. We are not really choosing between hope and despair, nor between togetherness and selfishness, nor between skill and incompetence. It is more like choosing between a sugar-coated doughnut and a chocolate-topped doughnut: important for doughnut lovers with strong feelings about sugar versus chocolate, but of little interest to people who don't like doughnuts in the first place.

PART IV
Inconsistently Popular

My friend Don plays the sought-after role of good listener. This allows him to determine what kind of man he should be: whether he should confess to a life-time concern for the welfare of panda bears and badgers or state with steely determination his intention to be a millionaire within two years.

It seems to work. Don is popular with women. The price is that he is forever contradicting himself, saying one thing to one woman and exactly the opposite to another. He is a Christian when it suits and an Atheist when it doesn't. He is a Socialist one day and a Capitalist the next. It is a price he is happy to pay. Don values popularity much higher than consistency.

Most politicians have the same values. Their jobs depend on being popular, not consistent. They have an interest in telling you what you want to hear. And, since not everyone wants to hear the same thing, like Don, they need to be flexible in their opinions.

But politicians face a problem that Don does not. Don chats women up in private. Tonight's audience has no idea that last night's heard a completely different tune. Politicians, however, must do their seducing in public. When a politician tells Daisy what she wants to hear, Maisy is listening too. It is difficult to then tell Maisy what she wants to hear without both Daisy and Maisy noticing the contradiction.

Difficult but not impossible. A skilful politician can tailor his opinions to the audience or the occasion without creating concern about their inconsistency. Usually, he can rely upon the vagueness of his language and the intellectual failings of his audience; people have short memories and hold inconsistent beliefs themselves. Sometimes, however, his opinions shift around or combine in such a peculiar way that anyone would be alarmed. Then he must employ special techniques to either obscure or justify his inconsistency. The following chapters discuss three such techniques. The first is widely practised; the next two are specialities of Mr Blair.

10 Universal Principles for Particular Occasions

Several of my secondary school teachers used to tell us that we should not generalise. They suggested that it was a sign of a simple mind. The world is too complex and varied for generalising to be a good idea. They normally shared this wisdom after some pupil had made an obnoxious remark, perhaps that women cannot drive or that all Nigerians are criminals.

But the problem with such statements is not that they are generalisations. It is that they are false. There is nothing wrong with true generalisations, such as that water boils at 100 degrees Celsius or that all men are mortal. Indeed, our teachers taught us many. Far from being something to avoid, generalisations are the ultimate goal of scientific enquiry. What could be more general than the laws of nature?

Nor should generalisations be avoided when arguing your case, if only because avoiding them is impossible. Suppose you claimed that someone should be put to death on the ground that he has been convicted of murder. Implicit in your argument is a generalisation: namely, that all convicted murderers should be put to death. If this generalisation were not true, then it would not follow from the fact that someone has been convicted of murder that he should be killed. Or suppose you claimed that fox hunting should be banned because it is cruel. Again, you implicitly invoke a generalisation: that cruel sports should be banned. Deny this generalisation and your argument against fox hunting collapses.

Since politicians are always making cases for their preferred policies, they cannot avoid generalisations. There is no shame in it. Nevertheless, they are reluctant to admit it and be open about the generalisations that their arguments implicitly invoke. For, as their name implies, generalisations apply generally: not just in the particular case under discussion but in all relevant cases. If cruel sports should be illegal then it isn't only fox hunting that is in trouble; shooting and fishing should also be banned, assuming these sports also cause animal suffering. The generalisation you invoke has implications well beyond the case where you apply it. And that is unfortunate. A politician may, for example, want to ban fox hunting but not shooting or fishing. Whereas there are many voters who oppose fox hunting and few who hunt foxes, there are many who fish and few who oppose fishing. Being open about the generalisation on which you base your opposition to fox hunting can only cause trouble when it comes to shooting and fishing.

As with fox hunting, so in general. You don't want your justification of one policy to land you with unwanted commitments elsewhere. Politicians are thus experts at evading the unwanted implications of the generalisations they cannot help but invoke. They have several techniques, as we shall see, but their favourite is simply to pretend that their positions are based on no general ideas at all.

*

Details and particulars are the best things behind which to hide general principles. A politician who can display a complete command of the facts of the case can make it seem that his position is based on no general ideas at all. He is simply advocating the policy that will work best in this particular case. He is the political equivalent of an engineer confronted with the knotty problem of how to make sure some ancient, sea battered bridge does not collapse. The right method of reinforcement depends on the particular circumstances of the bridge concerned.

Alas, this analogy reveals the fraudulence of the tactic. Knowing all the details of the case is never enough to know the right answer. An engineer may know the weight of the bridge, the type and volume of traffic that flows across it, the force of the waves beating against it and the rigidity of the materials from which it is built. But if he doesn't know some general rules – the relevant laws of physics, for example – he won't know what method of reinforcement will work best in these circumstances.

Despite its absurdity, most politicians are devoted to this 'it's all case specific' tactic. They refuse to be drawn on the general principles that lie behind their decisions on particular cases. That is why they refuse to answer hypothetical questions. Ask a question designed to draw out a politician's principles, such as 'if the Security Council did not sanction it, would you invade Iraq anyway?', and you will get the standard replies about the foolishness of speculating and the need to cross bridges only when we come to them. The Prime Minister's Official Spokesman has in fact declared that he does not answer hypothetical questions as a matter of policy.[28]

It seems to be Mr Blair's policy too. Here, for example, is an exchange between Mr Blair and Jeremy Paxman concerning the matter of what might be taught in the kind of 'faith-based' schools that Mr Blair favours:[29]

> *Paxman:* Is it appropriate, as a matter of principle,
> that creationism be taught in schools?
> *Blair:* But I am not sure that it is and therefore I don't
> know that it's a relevant question.
> *Paxman:* With respect, that's not the question.
> *Blair:* Well, it is, in the sense that there is no point in
> asking me a completely hypothetical question.
> *Paxman:* I'm not.

The point of asking a politician hypothetical questions is,
of course, to clarify his general principles. It is a perfectly
sensible thing to do. But in this case, Mr Blair was not asked
a hypothetical question, like 'if a school taught creationism
would you deny it government funding?' He was asked the
question of principle directly. By claiming that the question
was 'purely hypothetical' he meant to imply that the possibility in question was so remote that there is no point having
an opinion on the matter. But, if the possibility really were
remote, he would gladly have taken a strong stance, secure in
the knowledge that it would never be tested. It is precisely
because the possibility of faith-based schools teaching nonsense is very real that Mr Blair doesn't want to tell us what
he thinks about the issue. That would only tie his hands
should the eventuality arise.

*

Sometimes the general principles upon which a policy is
based are too obvious to hide, even with any amount of de-
tail. And people may point out other implications of the generalisation for which the politician does not care. In this case,
the trick is to add an irrelevant qualification that excludes
the unwanted implications.

We are all tempted to do this when we get caught giving a
bogus justification for some action, or inaction. Your aunt invites you to a weekend in the country that you fear might kill

you with boredom. You make your apologies on the ground that long car trips give you migraines.

'But you were on good form at Christmas, having just driven from Edinburgh,' she reminds you.

'Yes, yes, except during the festive season,' you add in your desperation. You have a very peculiar medical condition!

You would think it too obviously silly for a politician to do publicly. It isn't. In September 1999 Mr Blair sought to limit the political damage from his support for a ban on hunting with hounds. Writing in the *Daily Telegraph*, he reassured people who hunt without hounds:

> First, there will be no ban on the country pursuits of shooting and fishing. I know this is a matter of concern for many people, whether they live in the countryside or in our cities and towns. So let me make this perfectly clear. As long as I am Prime Minister, I guarantee that this Government will not allow any ban. We will not do it.[30]

But why not? The standard argument against fox hunting is that it is cruel to foxes. Or, as the Blairite Culture Secretary, Tessa Jowell, recently put it: the government supports 'the right of the majority to live in a humane, modern society, which does not treat the killing of animals as "sport"'.[31] But the sports of fishing and shooting involve the killing of animals. Surely they too should be illegal. What is the relevant difference between the cruel sport of hunting foxes with hounds and the cruel sports of shooting and fishing? Why should the former be outlawed and the latter protected at all political cost?

In his article Mr Blair hinted at an answer. He pointed out that hunting with hounds is a 'minority interest'. He could not have been suggesting a whole new principal of jurisprudence, that all minority interests should be illegal. That would rule out stamp collecting and running for political office, among other harmless activities. Rather, he must have been suggesting a qualification to the cruelty principle. He thinks that cruel minority sports should be illegal; popular forms of cruelty are just fine.

This qualification gets Mr Blair off the hook with regard to shooting and fishing, which, though minority interests, are more popular than fox hunting. The problem is that this modified principle is preposterous. If a cruel activity should be illegal when only a few people do it, surely there is even more reason to ban it when it is popular. It is hard to believe Mr Blair really believes his new principle. If torture became a popular pastime, would he support its decriminalisation? Of course, that is a purely hypothetical question that Mr Blair would therefore refuse to answer, but his position on fox hunting and fishing would seem to commit him to answering yes.

The fact that fox hunting is a minority interest is irrelevant to the question of whether or not the law should allow it. It is relevant only to the electoral implications of criminalising it. Banning minority pursuits loses only a few votes; banning fishing could be an election loser. It is surprising that someone who promised to ensure that 'justice has a high place at the cabinet table'[32] should so readily confuse what serves his interests with what is right.

*

When a politician's policy is popular he need not justify it. Such cases therefore involve no serious risk of any general ideas or principles being exposed. But not all policies are popular and then the risk is high, because it will be tempting to defend them by explicitly invoking a principle.

This happened recently with the government's proposal to change the gambling laws in a way that would allow so-called mega-casinos to operate in England and Wales. The idea met stiff resistance in the press. Tessa Jowell, Secretary of State for Culture, Media and Sport, responded by writing an article in *The Observer* about the issue of state paternalism versus individual liberty. She claimed that the government's regulations are guided by the principle that 'the freedom of adults to spend their time and money as they choose should be respected; autonomy is a right, not a privilege'.[33]

At about the same time, John Reid, the Health Secretary, endorsed this liberalism when defending his decision not to ban smoking altogether:

> You are free under the law to do things that risk your own health. What you are not allowed to do in a civilised society is things that damage the health of others and do things that cause discomfort to others.[34]

This was a thrilling time for those of us who think politicians should be more open about their guiding principles. But it was also reckless of Mr Reid and Ms Jowell. If their ideas really do represent the government's philosophy, it is not only gambling legislation that must be reformed. The laws that prevent people from taking recreational drugs also violate the above principles. Someone who snorts cocaine, for example, harms only himself. According to Mr Reid's principle, a civilised society ought to allow it.

Mr Reid has not proposed the legalisation of cocaine, and he is unlikely to in the foreseeable future. It would be a terrible gaffe: the kind for which he would almost certainly lose his cabinet position. Having made the blunder of stating a general principle, he is better off keeping his mouth shut about cocaine and quietly holding an inconsistent set of ideas. With any luck few will notice and even fewer will care.

In fact, not much luck will be required. The government

gets very little grief over the wild inconsistencies in its policies. Since his intellectual conversion, Mr Blair has claimed that free markets, competition and the profit motive are the best way to ensure an efficient allocation of resources. Why then does he not try to privatise the NHS and state schools? The answer cannot be that these services are too important to 'be left to the free market'. What could be more important than the production and distribution of food? Yet the Labour Party never suggests nationalising farms and supermarkets. Perhaps Mr Blair has some complex set of principles that explains why schools should be nationalised but not supermarkets. But if he does, he doesn't tell us what it is. In the meantime, he appears to have an incoherent set of policies.

Many think it is childishly pedantic to demand consistency from politicians. It shows a failure to understand the messy reality of politics. Politicians need to be masters of 'the art of the possible', not intellectual purists. Those of us who worry about consistency should grow up.

But consistency is not a matter of purely academic concern. If statements are inconsistent, then at least one of them is false. A politician who advocates policies that violate principles he uses to defend other policies isn't just intellectually corrupt; he has some wrong policies – at least, he does if his principles are true. If smoking and drinking should be allowed because they cause little harm to anyone but the smokers and drinkers, then snorting cocaine should be allowed too. The law preventing it is wrong. Improperly denying citizens their liberties is a serious mistake. It is not something that only pedants should worry about.

Many people buy their children pets as Christmas gifts only to tire of them a few weeks later and abandon them in the cold or take them to a vet to be killed. To discourage this, animal charities occasionally run a campaign with the slogan: 'A dog is for life, not just for Christmas.' Well, the same goes for principles: they are for all occasions, not just the convenient ones. Politicians should remember that before they adopt a principle that suits some policy they are promoting, only to abandon it few weeks later when trying to avoid one of its unwanted implications.

11 This Ever Changing World

No one likes changing his mind, for a simple reason: if your new opinion is true then your old opinion must have been false. To change your mind is to admit error.

People really shouldn't worry about it so much. There need be nothing shameful in changing your opinion. Intelligent, well-informed people get things wrong. And, when they discover they have, revising their opinions is the only sensible thing to do. Changing your mind occasionally should be taken as a virtue. It shows that you are still thinking about things. If you have held exactly the same opinions for the past ten years, then you know when your brain shut down.

Why then are politicians so reluctant to admit that they have changed their position on an issue? The obvious answer is that doing so creates a kerfuffle in the media. The politician will immediately be accused of making a U-turn. It is a strange accusation. Making a U-turn is, of course, prohibited on some busy streets, but usually it is a sensible thing to do when you discover you are travelling in the wrong direction.

The fuss made by the media is not always silly, however.

A politician's changing his position can sometimes be a bad sign. It might, for example, show that he is shifty. He may have had no new insight beyond recognising that his old opinions would not get him elected. The intellectual epiphanies of politicians, you will notice, tend to move them from less to more popular beliefs, and rarely in the other direction.

Even when a politician has genuinely changed his opinion, we still might not like what it reveals about him. We might think he was foolish to have been so wrong in the first place or that his recantation is glib. Only a light intellect is so easily blown around in the wind of ideas.

No politician wants to appear shifty or glib. So they normally try to minimise the impression of changing positions. Studied vagueness will often suffice. If you can't ever tell quite what a politician believes it is hard to know when he has changed his mind. When a political party changes its position, potentially awkward questions can be avoided by changing spokesman. That way, no one need explain his personal change of opinion. Since 1997 the Conservative Party has had many and diverse policies on funding higher education. But the difficult questions this might have raised have been largely avoided by having many and anonymous shadow education secretaries.

Sometimes, however, neither vagueness nor shuffling the cabinet will suffice. Sometimes the changes of position are so large and so obviously located in a single person that no one could fail to notice them. Mr Blair presented himself to the electorate in 1997 as a champion of free markets, friend of the business sector and dependable supporter of Britain's military commitments within NATO. This was quite a departure from the 1980s when Mr Blair had supported what was then Labour Party orthodoxy, including opposition to free markets, hostility towards private enterprise and even a policy of unilateral nuclear disarmament.

Mr Blair could not possibly deny the changes. Indeed, he advertised them, even changing the name of his party to New Labour. He publicly announced that the far-left policies of Old Labour had been abandoned in favour of his new improved Third Way policies. But how could he avoid either of the unwanted conclusions that such a large change of position must suggest to people: that it was not a genuine intellectual conversion but pure political expediency or that Mr Blair was very stupid ever to have believed all that leftwing stuff that he now told us was wrong?

Mr Blair had a simple solution. He told us that he had only changed his beliefs in accordance with the changes that had taken place in the world. His old beliefs were true when he had them. But things have changed and his new beliefs are true now.

*

During the 1997 election campaign, David Dimbleby grilled Mr Blair about his radical policy changes. Here are a few lines from their interview:

> *Dimbleby:* But did you believe in Old Labour?
> *Blair:* I believed in the values of the Labour Party, yes.
> *Dimbleby:* No, did you believe in what they stood for? Did you believe in CND? Did you believe in union power not being curtailed? Did you believe in nationalisation/no privatisation?
> *Blair:* There are a whole series of policy positions that I adopted along with the rest of the Labour Party. But the very process of modernisation has been the very process that I have undertaken in the Labour Party.
> *Dimbleby:* I know that – but have you abandoned ... did you believe what you said you believed in the 80s?

> *Blair:* Look, of course we always believed in the idea
> of a more just and more fair society. And the Labour
> Party believed for a long period of time that the way
> to do that was, for example, greater nationalisation,
> was, for example, simply more increased state spend-
> ing. The whole process of modernisation, David, has
> been to take the Labour Party away from that, to keep
> true to its principles, but put those principles prop-
> erly in a modern setting.
> *Dimbleby:* So all that was wrong.
> *Blair:* No, I don't say all that was wrong, I simply say
> what is important is to apply those principles to the
> modern world. Look, for example, John Major stood
> in the 1970s on a platform of Scottish devolution;
> Margaret Thatcher was the person that closed more
> grammar schools than anyone else. She was a mem-
> ber of Ted Heath's government. You know, times
> move on...[35]

Mr Blair here claims that his principles have remained the
same, but the world in which he must apply them has
changed. That is why his policies have changed. The fact that
he used to have different policies reveals no error in the past.
As he says, 'No, I don't say that was all wrong.'

Changing policies can sometimes reflect changing circumstances and hence no error in the original position. For example, in 1991 the International Rugby Board excluded South
Africa from the World Cup, but in 1995 it allowed South
Africa to host the event. This change implied no error in the
1991 exclusion. It was a case of 'same principles, different circumstances'. The policy of not playing rugby with a nation
that practices apartheid had not changed; South Africa had.

The idea that something similar explains the revision of
Mr Blair's policies, however, is ridiculous. To see this you
need only consider the topics on which he has changed his

opinion, such as the labour market. In 1987 Mr Blair favoured an inflexible, trades unions dominated labour market. In 1997 he favoured a flexible labour market where trades unions have limited powers of industrial action. According to Mr Blair his early position was not a mistake; in 1987 an inflexible Labour market was better. By 1997, however, the world had changed so that a flexible labour market was better.

Yet what was this change? What was the labour market equivalent of South Africa's rejection of apartheid? He never tells us. Did the laws of economics linking flexible labour markets to low unemployment come into existence some time in the early 1990s?

Or what about unilateral nuclear disarmament? How had the world changed between 1983 and 1997 to make that policy change from right to wrong? At first sight, Mr Blair seems to have got things exactly the wrong way around. In 1983 Britain was still involved in a 'cold war' with a major nuclear power. By 1997 there was no apparent threat that a large nuclear arsenal was required to repel.

The world may be changing rapidly, as Mr Blair never tires of telling us. But that doesn't mean he can move from one ideology to another without admitting error. Mr Blair has changed his mind about matters that transcend the particular circumstances of 1987 and 1997. If flexible labour markets were a good idea in 1997 then they were a good idea in 1987 too, as Margaret Thatcher then claimed. It is preposterous for Mr Blair to say that the changes in his beliefs only track changes in reality. In the areas where Mr Blair has changed his mind, the world doesn't change that much or that fast.

*

If Mr Blair's New Labour agenda was right in 1997 then his Old Labour agenda was wrong in 1987. Mr Blair should have the honesty to admit it. Such a plain admission, however, could only raise a difficult question: how could he have got things so wrong in the past?

When not flatly denying any error, Mr Blair hints at a standard defence: that in making this mistake he was no different from anyone else. Or, as he put it to David Dimbleby: 'There are a whole series of policy positions that I adopted along with the rest of the Labour Party.'

The idea is not, I hope, that a crime is mitigated if you commit it as part of a gang. Rather, it is that, given the state of human knowledge in the 1980s, espousing Old Labour ideology was a mistake that a reasonable man might make: that's what everyone thought back then.

It can be reasonable to believe things that turn out to be false. Most physicists in 1900 believed that the mass of an object does not vary with its velocity. If Einstein's 1905 Special Theory of Relativity is true, then they were wrong about this. But we do not conclude that these physicists were intellectual lightweights, because in 1900 they had no reason to believe that an object's mass increases with its velocity.

Alas, we cannot take the same generous attitude towards believing Old Labour ideology in 1987. It was not then a mistake made by most intelligent and well-informed people. On the contrary, so few people any longer adhered to far-left doctrine that the Labour Party had become unelectable, as Mr Blair has publicly recognised.

Mr Blair's early 1990s ideological conversion does not make him the equivalent of one of those early 20th century physicists who was quick to recognise Einstein's breakthrough and openly abandon his old Newtonian ideas. There was no such breakthrough in economics between 1987 and 1997. Mr Blair is more like the head of the world's last Newtonian physics department who decided to go Einsteinian only when he realised that otherwise no students would enrol.

12 Eat Your Cake

Life is full of unpleasant choices. Will you eat that chocolate or have a slim waste? Will you sleep with your secretary or stay married? Will you indulge yourself now or save
for your old age?

How you wish you could transcend these dreadful trade-
offs. How you wish you could have it both ways: chocolate
and beauty, fun when young and old, promiscuity and a stable marriage.

Well, now you can! That is what people will always tell
you. They have made a breakthrough that can liberate you
from the old choices, which they will share with you for a
small fee. Send £12.99 for your copy of *Eat Yourself Slim*.
Invest just £20 a week in our amazing fund and watch it grow
into millions in just a few years. Sign up to *Alibis R Us* and
sleep around with impunity.

Not only charlatans make such claims. Sometimes these
breakthroughs are real. Low-calorie sweeteners mean you
can now drink as much Coke as you like, albeit Diet Coke,
without getting fat. The jet aeroplane means you can now

travel from England to Australia without spending months at sea. With the contraceptive pill women can enjoy sex without fearing pregnancy. Science has delivered us from many past trade-offs.

Mr Blair claims to have made such a breakthrough in politics:

> Over the last seven years New Labour has time and again shown how ideas that are supposed to be irreconcilable can be brought together: social justice and economic efficiency; fairness at work and a flexible labour market; full employment and low inflation.[36]

This marriage of what had formerly been thought irreconcilable is Mr Blair's Third Way. It combines the best of the Old Left, such as social justice, with the best of the New Right, such as economic efficiency. The Third Way transcends the old duality of Left and Right.

Who will ignore such a breakthrough? Who will turn his back on the best of both worlds? Only reactionaries, from both the Left and the Right, will resist Mr Blair's ideological revolution. Just tick this box and get with the programme.

Alas, Mr Blair's Third Way is not quite the breakthrough he claims.

*

Suppose I told you that I had discovered that salt and pepper are not really inconsistent after all. Behold this beef stew! It contains both salt and pepper. You would be unimpressed. No one thought salt and pepper were irreconcilable in the first place.

That is the first problem with Mr Blair's self-declared achievement. Consider social justice and economic efficiency. The meaning of 'social justice' is unclear. It might simply mean justice. 'Social' seems to be an empty qualification of the word 'justice'. What, after all, is anti-social justice? But if social justice is simply justice, then who could ever have thought it inconsistent with economic efficiency? The economic efficiency of developed nations is founded upon the rule of law and enforceable contracts provided by their judicial systems. This has been well understood for centuries. To suggest that, prior to the advent of New Labour, conventional wisdom had considered justice and economic efficiency to be at odds is outrageously stupid.

Of course, by 'social justice' Mr Blair might not mean justice. He might mean what many on the Left mean by it: namely, redistribution of wealth. But if this is what he means then social justice and economic efficiency really are at odds, even now that we have New Labour.

Taxation creates what economists call deadweight losses. These are losses that are not offset by any corresponding gain. Deadweight loss is economic inefficiency. The greater the deadweight loss, the greater the inefficiency. Taxes create this economic inefficiency because they discourage people from engaging in the taxed activity, such as earning income or purchasing goods. Head or 'poll' taxes are an exception because they cannot be avoided by changing your economic behaviour. Only killing yourself will suffice, and that defeats the purpose of avoiding tax, which is normally better to enjoy your money, not just to thwart the government.

Mr Blair has not found a way of redistributing wealth that does not require taxation. Nor has he discovered a way to avoid the deadweight losses of taxation. So he has not found a way of avoiding the trade-off between economic efficiency and the redistribution of wealth.

Britain now has an economy that is relatively efficient by international standards while also redistributing wealth. But no one should confuse making a trade-off with transcending it. All developed countries have tax systems that reduce economic efficiency for the sake of redistributing wealth. Some, such as Sweden, tax and redistribute more. Others, such as the United States, tax and redistribute less. New Labour has moved Britain slightly in the direction of Sweden, increasing tax and government spending. But nothing transcendent has occurred. Moving along a spectrum is not the same as moving off it.

The same goes for fairness at work and a flexible labour market. On a common understanding of fairness, there is no apparent tension. I know many who think it perfectly fair that an employer should set any conditions of employment he likes. No one is obliged to work for him. On this view, fairness at work and a flexible labour market are the same thing.

Only if you understand 'fairness at work' to mean employee protection is there any apparent tension. And the tension is not just apparent. A minimum wage, employer National Insurance contributions and minimum notice periods really do make a labour market less flexible. There is nothing Mr Blair can do to stop it. Even God couldn't stop it, anymore than He could stop the addition of weight making something heavier.

Britain now has a flexible labour market compared to Germany, for example. But that is precisely because it has less employee protection. Again, Mr Blair confuses making some specific trade-off with transcending the trade-off altogether.

Eating only a little chocolate and being just a bit chubby is not a way of transcending the choice between chocolate and beauty. Nor can you avoid the choice between spending and saving by spending a little less. But you can see why people are tempted to pretend that such compromises are in fact great breakthroughs. A breakthrough makes for a better sales pitch. 'Now you can eat your cake and have it too' sounds like real progress. 'Now you can eat a bit of your cake and have some left over' is less impressive, especially since everyone always knew they could.

*

In the speech quoted above, Mr Blair reminded his audience of his excellent track record in reconciling the irreconcilable because he was announcing his intention to do it again. This time he was going to reconcile the choice and quality characteristic of goods and services supplied through the private sector with the state provision of public services, such as health and education. As Mr Blair put it:

> The service will continue to be free, but it will be a high quality consumer service to fit their needs in the same way as the best services do in other areas of life.[37]

Mr Blair hopes that by introducing more consumer choice into public services – for example, by increasing the number of subjects available on the National Curriculum and giving patients a wider choice of hospitals – he can achieve for the public services the same level of customer satisfaction enjoyed by supermarkets, footwear manufacturers and the other success stories of the private sector.

This time Mr Blair is not making his usual mistake. He is not confusing making a trade-off with avoiding one. Rather, he is attempting to overcome the laws of economics. Which is why his planned reconciliation cannot work. Choice cannot solve the customer satisfaction problems that beset the public services while they remain free to consumers.

To see this, imagine a country where the state provides wine free to drinkers, funded from tax revenues. What will happen? Since its consumption costs nothing, demand for wine is unlimited. Supply, however, is not. So wine must be rationed. Choice and quality must be restricted too; taxpayers cannot fund Chateau Petrus for all. Drinkers find themselves in long queues to receive bog-standard wine from their local state-run off-licence.

Except the wealthy, who increasingly buy wine from a few private off-licences, where a wide range of wines is readily available, at a price. People become unhappy with the quantity and quality of wine available through the National Wine Service (NWS).

Will the problem be solved by increasing consumer choice, by lengthening the National Wine List and the range of NWS off-licenses from which each drinker may shop? Not on its own. The problems of the NWS arise because the Government cannot match supply to demand. It does not know how much to spend on wine nor which wines to supply to whom. Answering these questions requires consumer choice, but also prices.

Do you prefer a bottle of Jacob's Creek at £5 or a bottle of Chateau Petrus at £500? That depends on how rich you are but also on how much you care about wine. A millionaire may prefer Jacob's Creek because he would rather spend the £495 that he has saved on something else. The right supply of Chateau Petrus and Jacob's Creek depends on how consumers make such trade-offs.

Remove prices, however, and the optimal supply cannot be determined. When everything costs consumers the same – in this case, nothing – consumers will always choose the best available. If Chateau Petrus and Jacob's Creek were both free, everyone would want lots of the former and none of the latter. Petrus would have to be rationed, and Jacob's Creek forced on disgruntled drinkers.

Where consumers pay nothing, state rationing is unavoidable. As consumers, people want rations increased; as taxpayers, they want them decreased. The state ration imposes a trade-off between these conflicting desires. Where there are prices, however, consumers ration themselves. The advantage of prices over tax-funded free consumption is that individuals know their preferred trade-offs better than the state can. That is why consumers are typically more satisfied with goods and services they receive via the private sector than those they receive from the state.

Perhaps Mr Blair has an answer for this apparent problem, a breakthrough idea that eliminates the need for prices in efficiently allocating resources. If he has, he should share it with us, if only because it would be worth a Nobel prize in economics. Until he does, however, it can only seem that Mr Blair is attempting the impossible.

Many will be impressed to hear that Mr Blair is attempting to do the impossible. Because nothing is really impossible. 'Impossible' is just a word for people who aren't willing to put in 110% effort.

Or who won't put their faith in New Labour. Never mind what the economics books say. Wouldn't it be wonderful if everybody could enjoy the choice and excellence offered within the private schools sector but without having to pay? Wouldn't it be great if you could increase taxation and unemployment benefits without discouraging people from working? Wouldn't it be heavenly if employees could be offered every legal protection without making employers reluctant to hire them? Oh brother, don't let doubt keep you from the promised land.

PART V

Haven't We Done Well?

You needn't do much when you're young, except show potential. That will get you all the admiration and financial support you need. As you age, however, people expect to see your potential backed up by some results. They start to look not at what you might do but at what you have in fact done. That is part of what makes growing up so horrible.

The same goes for governments. When they are newly elected and fresh-faced it is all about promise. And the electorate, having just taken the plunge with them, is keen to believe their promises, allowing politicians to indulge in extraordinary optimism about the new age heralded by their election. In 1997 Mr Blair promised that:

> Together you and I will begin to build the new society, a society in which each of us has the chance to grow, to achieve, to contribute, to create dignity for ourselves, and not for ourselves alone, but for others

also; a society in which each of us has a stake, a share and we will give back to our children what they deserve – a heritage of hope.[38]

New societies do not arrive just like that, of course. It takes more than a few months to establish a heritage of hope. So this kind of rhetoric can be enjoyed for quite some time. But not forever. People have limited patience. Even Jesus told his followers that he would return to establish paradise on earth while they still lived.[39] And modern men are not nearly as patient or as gullible as first century Christians. It takes only a few years before they get tired of hearing about the promised New Jerusalem and start asking what the government has actually achieved.

That is why Mr Blair's speeches now typically include several paragraphs on the achievements of his government. Perhaps they do not amount to a whole new society – who could ever have expected that? – but Mr Blair believes they are impressive. In June 2004, for example, he claimed that:

In seven years, we have delivered a stable economy, rising employment, and big reductions in unemployment and poverty.[40]

A politician may be forgiven such open self-congratulation; the opposition is unlikely to advertise his achievements. But even a politician should stick to the basic rules of boasting. He should not take credit for others' achievements, he should not pretend that failures are successes and he should not exaggerate his achievements.

The following three chapters concern the ways Mr Blair breaks these rules. Many of the achievements he claims for himself are in fact achievements of the previous Conservative government or simply the result of good luck. Others are not necessarily achievements at all but only appear to be because Mr Blair fails to mention their costs, or even counts their costs as benefits. Then there is Mr Blair's habit of mistaking trying and succeeding; he boasts about mere government activity, as if there could be no doubt that it will benefit us.

13 Taking Credit

Designing a bonus scheme for a chief executive officer (CEO) is difficult. A CEO is supposed to work in the interests of the shareholders, doing a good job if he increases the market value of the company and a bad job otherwise. You might think the obvious answer is to link his bonus to changes in the company's market value: say, £1 in bonus for every £100 of additional market value.

But this obvious answer is wrong. It assumes that the CEO is responsible for any change in his company's market value. He isn't. The value of a steel company, for example, will vary with the global demand for steel and with the price of raw materials, neither of which is controlled by the CEO. If the price of iron ore drops and profits increase, that is good luck, not good performance. It is no reason to reward the CEO.

Precisely how to measure a CEO's contribution is a knotty question, and one that creates plenty of work for 'compensation consultants'. But we need not worry about the answer here, beyond noting that it would be foolish to give a CEO credit for every increase in his company's value.

Yet that is precisely what Mr Blair would have us do when it comes to assessing the performance of his government. He simply lists pleasing facts about Britain during his term in office and invites us to conclude that he has done a good job. The economy is a favourite. In his 2004 Labour party conference speech he pointed to:

> ... the longest period of economic growth since records began, an economy now bigger than that of Italy and France. The lowest unemployment and highest employment rate of any of our competitors for the first time since the 1950s.

And he concluded on the basis of this evidence alone that 'Labour is working'.

Yet we should conclude that Labour is working only if these economic facts are the result of Labour Party policies. The simple fact that they have occurred during Labour's term in office does not show that they are. Just as a steel company's share price may rise six months after the appointment of a new CEO without his being the cause of it, so economic prosperity during a Labour term in office need not be caused by Labour's policies. To argue, as Mr Blair does, directly from coincidence to causation is to commit a simple fallacy: the *cum hoc ergo propter hoc* fallacy (the *with this therefore because of this* fallacy). Events may coincide without being cause and effect.

Politicians never forget this when things go wrong, blaming years of Tory (or Labour) mismanagement, a global recession, rising oil prices or anything except themselves. They forget it only when things are going well. But it is true in good times as well as bad. If a politician wants the credit for our economic prosperity, or for anything else, he must tell us how he brought it about. It isn't enough simply to observe that it has occurred. Otherwise, why should we not also thank him when the sun shines?

*

By merely identifying rather than explaining attractive facts about present day Britain, Mr Blair fails properly to make his case that Labour is working. Of course, this failure does not mean the case could not be made. Perhaps Mr Blair has spent hours at Number 10 convincing himself, with detailed analysis, that everything good really is the outcome of Labour policies. He doesn't share the analysis with us only because he fears it would bore us. Perhaps his apparent leaps of logic reflect only a good communicator's desire to leave out the tedious details.

This may sometimes explain it. But we cannot, in general, give Mr Blair the benefit of this doubt. He takes credit for too many achievements that really are not his own. Our current prosperity is a perfect example.

Britain's growing prosperity since the early 1990s has three principal causes: the UK's competitive market-economy (especially the flexibility of its labour market), the effective use of interest rates to manage domestic demand, and increasing global prices for the knowledge-based services provided by British businesses relative to the manufactured goods produced in developing countries, such as China and Korea. The first is a legacy of Mrs Thatcher's deregulation, privatisation and trade union reform. The second is the result of the UK's removal from the Exchange Rate Mechanism in 1991.* The

---

*Mr Blair often claims that granting independence to the Bank of England in 1997 accounts for the improvements in interest rate management. Central bank independence is desirable because it stops governments lowering interest rates to create an inflationary pre-election consumer boom. But this effect is small compared with changing the goal of monetary policy from managing

third is a consequence of technological advances and globalisation. None is the result of Labour Party policy.

Such economic explanations are contentious and I have made no case for this one.[41] But it is not an eccentric view of the matter and Mr Blair offers no alternative explanation on which his government's actions are decisive. On the contrary, he tacitly agrees. He made it clear from the start that New Labour's economic policy was aimed primarily at not wrecking the golden legacy they inherited when they came to power in 1997. He consistently reassured nervous voters that he had no intention of unravelling the Conservatives' economic reforms. He even promised to stick to Tory spending plans for his first two years in government.

Of course, some credit should be given to those who do not blow their inheritance. But not much, and certainly less than is due to those who created it. No one would be impressed to hear Bill Gates' children taking credit for their family's wealth, even if they show restraint in their personal spending. If they are honest they will give the glory to their father, and I expect they do. Such honesty is harder for politicians, however, especially when the credit is due, not to predecessors from their own party, but to the opposition.

Taking credit for the effects of the Conservatives' economic reforms might be tolerable if the Labour government had continued them. In many cases, however, its policies have worked against the Conservative reforms. Consider labour market flexibility, the virtues of which both Mr Blair and the chancellor, Mr Brown, so often extol.

---

the exchange rate to managing domestic demand. This important change took place under the Conservatives, not Labour. That said, it was forced upon the Conservatives by currency speculators' 1991 attack on Sterling. We should thank George Soros, not John Major.

The New Labour government has done three notable things to the UK Labour market. It has introduced a minimum wage, enacted many employee protection laws and extended workplace training to the long-term unemployed through the New Deal.

The effects of the New Deal and its cost efficiency are disputed, but it should increase labour market flexibility. A better-trained labour force is more able to adapt to changes in the demand for labour. The minimum wage and employee protection legislation, however, make the labour market less flexible. A minimum wage prevents wages dropping in line with the demand for labour and, by driving up the cost of employing someone, employee protection laws make employers reluctant to hire.

You may be in favour of a minimum wage and of increased employee protection but it cannot be because they help to make the labour market more flexible. Perhaps the unemployment caused by this inflexibility is a price worth paying for the benefits to employed workers. Then that is what Mr Blair should boast about, not the flexibility of Britain's labour markets, which Labour's policies have mainly reduced.

When wondering whether or not to give the sitting government credit for something, it is worth bearing in mind how long it takes for policies to have their effects. Some work very quickly. Introducing a £5 fee for driving in central London will reduce traffic volumes immediately. Less immediate is the effect of changing interest rates on consumer spending; it takes from six months to a year. And some policies take many years or even decades to work: for example, those aimed at creating the 'enterprise culture' that Mr Blair and Mr Brown boast about. Insofar as Britain has such a culture, it cannot be due to Labour party policies. They simply haven't had time to change British culture.

*

It isn't only Mr Blair who commits the *cum hoc ergo propter hoc* fallacy. All politicians do, for a very democratic reason.

To avoid the fallacy, you need to indulge in some theorising. Have Labour's policies increased or decreased unemployment? The question cannot properly be answered without some economic theory. Simply observing that unemployment has declined is not enough. Perhaps the decline would have been greater if not for Labour's policies. The same goes for all policy areas. You cannot explain why the policies you favour will have, or have had, the desired effects without appealing to relevant theories, be they about economics, climate change or traffic flows.

Indeed, you cannot even identify desirable effects without some theory. Suppose a politician seeks nothing but to improve people's lives. What does it mean to improve someone's life? That he is richer? That he has more free time? That he is more likely to go to heaven when he dies? The question cannot sensibly be avoided, despite the fact that it always is. And the answer will be as theoretical as you can get: namely, philosophical.

Alas, engaging in theory does not fit the political temperament of modern Britain. Not only are most voters too intellectually lazy for it, they don't trust it. A politician who stood up and began to explain his tax policies along the lines that an economist might think about them would be thought not just boring but tricky. Why is he trying to bamboozle us with all this mumbo jumbo? Just stick to the facts! Mr Blair's approach, on the contrary, has the appealing air of common sense. No dodgy economic theory; only the plain facts about what has actually happened.

Nor will oppositions risk looking sophistical by challenging on theoretical grounds the sitting government's claimed achievements. Instead, they allow the government its luck and hope it will turn. While the economy booms, the opposition must grin and bare it. When it tanks, the opposition will blame the government whether or not they can properly show the government to be responsible. This is not only intellectually bankrupt, it puts oppositions in the perverse position of wishing ill upon the country they love.

Whatever motivates the *cum hoc ergo propter hoc* fallacy, when politicians discuss the effects of policies you will rarely hear anything else. The government will merely list attractive facts from its time in power, while the opposition will list unattractive facts. So they waste our time. These facts may delight or appal us, but that isn't enough to show what caused them. Nor, therefore, which party or policies we should prefer.

14 Benefit Benefit Analysis

You cannot properly recommend an action by listing its benefits. Because all actions, no matter how stupid, have benefits. Even poking yourself in the eye with a fork has some, such as sympathy and time off work. Or consider a business scheme that involves selling for £50 a product that costs £100 to produce. It has its upside: namely the £50 per sale.

Properly to recommend an action, you need to show that its benefits exceed its costs. In other words, you need to show that, when the costs are subtracted from the benefits, the action remains in credit. The action must deliver a net-benefit.

Spending £100 to receive £50 obviously fails this test. And, for all but the strangest people, so does forking yourself in the eye. The pleasure of receiving sympathy and having a day off work does not adequately compensate for the pain.

Everyone understands this net-benefit principle. We all employ it unconsciously in the countless decisions we make every day: when we decide to put off walking the dog on account of the rain, or to have a bottle of wine despite the cost and health risk, or to just put the fork down and not poke ourselves in the eye. And businessmen employ it consciously when they conduct cost-benefit analyses of proposed new ventures. The net-benefit principle should hardly need mentioning, except for the fact that politicians consistently forget it. They try to recommend their policies by simply listing their benefits.

In July 2004, for example, Mr Blair recommended his government's massively increased spending on public services as follows:

> Let me pause to say what that year on year investment means. In health, it means a budget now doubled from £33bn in 1997 to £67bn this year, and set to rise to £90bn by 2008, bringing our health spending towards the European average for the first time in a generation. This is enabling us to recruit 20,000 more doctors, 68,000 more nurses and 26,000 more therapy, scientific and technical staff. In education it means a budget nearly doubled, from £30bn to £53bn, again bringing us towards international standards with 29,000 extra teachers in our schools.[42]

He goes on to list benefits in policing and housing, the details of which I will spare you. But never does he get around to the downside. He fails to mention that all these billions being spent on teachers and nurses are not a gift from a foreign nation or an anglophile oil sheikh. Their source is massively increased taxation.

Since Labour came to power in 1997, taxation has increased by about 25%, from £360 billion to £455 billion.[43] And, since the government is currently spending more than it receives in tax revenues, we can expect to pay yet more tax in the future.

It should not need stating, but, given the strange sentiments the issue arouses nowadays, perhaps it does: tax is a cost to those who pay it. To believe this you needn't agree with those libertarians who think that tax violates our absolute property rights, nor hold any other strange or obnoxious views. You need only believe something obviously true: that if your tax increases by £1, you have £1 less to spend. You are £1 worse off. Increasing your tax is no different from cutting your income, or increasing the cost of the goods you buy, which no one will deny represents a cost to you.

Since government spending is funded from taxation, the question is never simply whether we are glad to receive what the spending pays for. Rather, it is whether what we receive is worth the cost. Of course we are glad to have more teachers and nurses. But does their value exceed the billions of pounds of extra tax we are paying for them? Mr Blair never even tries to answer such questions.

On the contrary, he presents the spending as if it were itself the benefit. Look, we are spending £34 billion more on healthcare and £23 billion more on education! Aren't you glad?

Private spending is something you should be glad about, because it normally delivers a net-benefit. If I buy something for £1, then I must value it more than the £1 I spent on it; otherwise I would have been unwilling to pay £1 for it. Whoever sold it to me is also better off. He must have valued the item less than £1 to be willing to make the swap. Where government spending is concerned, however, there is no reason to assume it will deliver a net-benefit, because government spending severs the connection between paying and deciding what to buy.

Suppose, though unlikely, that you gave me access to your bank account and told me that I should take care of all your purchases for you. I would almost certainly buy you many things you don't want or, at least, that you value less than the money I spent on them. Even if I occasionally asked you roughly the kind of thing you were looking for, I would still often fail to make your preferred purchases. Given this, you should fear my spending rather than rejoice in it. You know that it will be wasteful: that, on average, £1 of my spending will give you stuff you value less than £1. Your heart should sink rather than swell when I gleefully announce that this month I have spent bucketloads of your money.

Where spending is outsourced it is unlikely to deliver a net-benefit. So Mr Blair ought to go to unusual lengths to show that, in the case of his public services policy, the benefits of this spending really do exceed the costs. Instead, he simply asks us to rejoice at the very scale of the spending, as if there were not the least risk of its being wasteful.

*

When discussing increased government spending, Mr Blair almost confuses a cost with a benefit. On the issue of employment, he succeeds.

Mr Blair often boasts that not only has his government reduced unemployment, it has increased employment. In his 2004 Labour Party conference speech he announced:

> ... the longest period of economic growth since records began ... The lowest unemployment and highest employment rate of any of our competitors for the first time since the 1950s.

The claim is not as vacuous as it might at first appear. Unemployment can decrease without employment increasing. Someone is unemployed when he wants work but has none. There are thus two ways to stop being unemployed: find work or stop wanting to. When I retire to live off the royalties from this book, I will not be unemployed.

Unemployment is an evil because the unemployed lack

something they want. Moving people from unemployment to employment benefits them. But otherwise increasing the number who are employed is of less obvious merit. It all depends on why people enter the workforce.

Consider me in six months time enjoying my early retirement sitting on a deck chair in Bermuda. My mobile phone rings and, by the end of the call, I have decided to re-enter the workforce. Has the world changed for the better? That depends on what explains my decision. If it was Mr Blair on the phone offering me a huge salary to take over as his Head of Strategic Communications, then working again marks an improvement in my fortunes. Rejoice. If, however, it was my stock broker on the phone telling me that the value of my share portfolio has collapsed, then my decision to re-enter the workforce only shows how wrong the world has gone.

Presbyterians may like working but most people do not. That is why they need to be paid to do it. Your job gives you a salary, friends and eight hours a day away from the family. These are the benefits that offset the cost of the actual toil. If you made a breakthrough in your productivity, so that you could generate the same income with half the effort, you would have an interesting decision to make. Should you work just as hard for twice the money, or work half as hard for the same money, or something in between? Those who value money higher than leisure will keep their heads down; those who value their free time higher will put their feet up.

The same goes for an entire economy. As productivity improves, the population can press on and deliver a larger Gross Domestic Product (GDP). Or the nation could make do with its current GDP and people could take it a little easier. Those of us who favour the second option will be accused of promoting an ethos of sloth. Perhaps. But as far as I know the seven deadly sins are not ranked: sloth is no worse than greed.

Whichever way you are inclined, however, you cannot do what Mr Blair does and count both increased GDP and increased employment as benefits in an economy. Working more is a price we pay for our increased GDP, not an additional benefit.

*

Mr Blair systematically fails to provide proper cost-benefit analyses of his policies. Who knows why? But even if he wanted to, he would find it difficult. I do not mean to call his intelligence into question. The problem is not Mr Blair's arithmetic but his policies. They make cost-benefit analysis close to impossible.

Cost-benefit analysis requires a common, numeric measure for the costs and the benefits. Without one you cannot subtract the former from the latter to discover whether the action produces a net-benefit. That is why those lists of pros and cons that people draw up when trying to make a difficult decision are useless. You might have twenty pros and only one con. But that doesn't mean you should take the action in question, because the one con might outweigh all the pros put together. Without values assigned to the pros and cons, your list cannot tell you what you should do.

Economists have a solution for this problem: that is, a way of assigning values to the pros and cons of any action or policy. They are valued by your willingness to pay for them or, in the case of cons, to avoid them. Suppose you are considering a new job and that one of its cons is that you will have to spend an hour longer commuting each day. What is the negative value of this con? It is what you would be willing to pay to avoid the extra travelling. One of the pros, let's suppose, is the prestige of being appointed a vice president. This is worth what you would be willing to pay for the title or, putting it the other way around, how much extra salary you would demand if denied it. Once you have assigned values to all the pros and cons, via this 'willingness to pay' method, you can sum them up. If the result is a positive number, then taking the job delivers a net-benefit: you should do it.

In theory, the same could be done for government policies. Take all the pros and cons for every individual affected, value them according to each individual's willingness to pay, then sum them up and see if you get a positive number. In practice, however, the government does not know what each individual would be willing to pay for the public services it provides. Nor, therefore, does it know whether these services are valued higher than the cost of the taxes required to fund them.

If individuals purchased healthcare and education directly out of their own cash, including cash received from the government, there would be no cause for concern. As already noted, people will buy something only if they value it higher than its price: only if its benefits exceed its cost. It is only because Mr Blair favours policies whereby the government buys healthcare and education on our behalf that he needs to know how highly we value it. And also why he does not know the answer. In a free market, you can tell how people value goods by what they actually pay for them. No such information is available, however, when goods are provided free to consumers. For a man who claims to favour markets, Mr Blair is strangely reluctant to take advantage of them in education and healthcare.

*

Mr Blair is not alone in this reluctance. The three main political parties in Britain all favour using tax revenues to fund services that are provided free to consumers. They may recommend different levels of spending, but since none knows what we would willingly pay for these services, none can know the right amount to spend. All must proceed on a mere hunch that the services they would provide are worth the cost.

In reality, the hunch on which they proceed is probably rather different. It is not that the benefits of their spending exceed the cost in tax. It is that the policy will gain more votes than it loses. And, when it comes to government spending, this calculation tends to favour increasing it, for two reasons.

The first is that the benefits of increased spending are typically enjoyed by many voters while the costs are borne by a few. Improving the quality of state education, for example, benefits 90 percent of families with school aged children. But the increased tax burden falls disproportionately on the rich: 50 percent of income tax is contributed by 10 percent of taxpayers. The policy has more winners than losers, even if the total cost exceeds the total benefit. Given our one-man one-vote system, any policy that has many small winners and a few big losers is likely to be a vote winner.

The second reason is that many voters now seem to believe that taxation is intrinsically good. They favour it even when they believe it will fund wasteful spending. In November 2002, an ICM poll asked voters if they were willing to pay more tax to fund increased spending on public services. 62 percent said yes. It also asked respondents if they believed this extra spending would improve standards in health and education. Only 51 percent said yes. At least eleven percent of voters favour pointless increases in taxation.

With such people in the electorate it is little wonder that Mr Blair promotes his policies on the ground that they are expensive. But that doesn't make the argument any better. Even in a democracy, pandering to fools is not the path to enlightenment.

15 Busy, Busy, Busy

One of my school friends had a very busy mother. I knew she was busy because she was in the habit of telling me what she had been doing recently. Each item on her list was of little interest in itself: making sandwiches, ironing shirts, cleaning windows, that sort of thing. But her lists were long and by the time she was about half way through it was difficult not to have fallen into an awe-struck stupor. When she concluded by declaring that she was utterly worn out, you could only share her pain.

Sympathy was not all she sought. I think she also hoped that her audience would admire her industry. For a brief period I was drawn in. I began to think ill of my own mother, who, between 3pm and 5pm, was usually to be found on the sofa eating chocolates while reading something unimproving. Yet our home was tidier than my friend's, our meals better, our shirts more crisply ironed. Ian's mother really did seem busier than mine but all this effort had no apparent effect on what got done. What my mother lacked in industry she more than made up for in efficiency.

Boasting about how hard you work is a peculiar thing to do. Unless all this effort is accompanied by extraordinary achievements, it can only make you look inefficient or incompetent. All undergraduates understand this. That is why they cultivate an image of self-indulgent indolence. If you took them at their word, their terms are occupied entirely by drinking, sex and dealing with the after-effects of these activities. The upper second class degree they ultimately achieve is testimony to their innate brilliance and an ability to extract the most out of an hour's hungover cramming on the morning of the exam. Undergraduates realise that, after kindergarten, there are no marks for effort.

Mr Blair does not. He seems to think people should be impressed to hear about the sheer volume of actions taken by his government. We are forever being told about new targets, new initiatives and new regulations. This New Labour government is incredibly busy. And Mr Blair is proud of the fact.

Some commentators have protested that Mr Blair's government tries to create an impression of being busier than it really is, by announcing the same initiative or budget allocation on several occasions. Or by mentioning mere flights of fancy as if they were serious policy proposals.

This is quibbling. No one can seriously doubt the industry of New Labour. Never has a government had such a clear or detailed idea of how we should live. It is a rare activity which this government does not either ban or require, or tax or subsidise, or advertise or admonish. Nothing more scandalises New Labour than the discovery of something that wants for its oversight and guidance.

The question is not whether New Labour really is busy; it must be worn out. The question is whether this is anything to boast about. Should we be glad about all this activity? Good results are welcome, of course, but why simple activity? To rejoice we would need to believe that government actions generally have their intended effects. This is not obviously true but we cannot get into the debate between the *laissez faire* and activist approaches to government here. Let's grant Mr Blair this contentious activist assumption. That still isn't enough to celebrate government activity. We also need to believe that it is intended to benefit us.

*

I once had a student who broke the general rule of indolence. When preparing his essays, he always went well beyond the recommended reading list. He let me see all this industry in his very long essays which contained digressions on the ideas he had encountered in his extra-curricular reading. Alas, all this effort contributed nothing to the task at hand: namely, answering the essay question. That was not its purpose. It was intended only to impress me.

Much New Labour activity has the same purpose. It is aimed not at achieving an outcome beneficial to us but simply at impressing us: that is, at achieving an outcome beneficial to New Labour.

In July 2000, a memo from Mr Blair to his ministers was leaked to the press. It was revealing about the way he approaches policy formulation. In the period leading up to the memo, the leader of the opposition, William Hague, had been making headway in the press with ideas about tougher immigration legislation and extending the rights of people to protect themselves against criminals. Mr Blair's memo demanded that his ministers respond with some 'eye-catching initiatives'. These initiatives should make New Labour appear pro-family and tough on crime, and Mr Blair 'should be personally associated with as much of this as possible'. He even made some specific policy proposals, including this one:

> We should think now of an initiative, e.g. locking up
> street muggers. Something tough, with immediate bite
> which sends a message through the system. Maybe,
> the driving licence penalty for young offenders.

Mr Blair and his ministers seem to approach public policy like advertising executives 'brainstorming' over lunch at The Ivy: 'Alistair really loved the extra-year-on-every-conviction special offer. He thinks it will get a lot of takers among Cs and Ds. Keep up the good work David.'

'Thanks Tony. Just wait till you see what we've got lined up for Christmas!'

The initiatives' effects on crime are irrelevant. There isn't time to work it out and that is not their purpose anyway. They are simply instruments for swaying public opinion.

It must be this marketing approach that has given us policies such as bribing delinquents to behave themselves with music vouchers[44] or reducing crime by forcing acting lessons on the children of prison inmates.[45] These ideas catch the eye but it is hard to imagine that ministers genuinely believe in their efficacy.

If an initiative were the result of serious efforts to determine what will lead to improvements in our lives, we might be pleased to hear about it. But why should we celebrate activities aimed solely at catching our attention, at creating an impression that the government is on top of things? They are intended not to help us but to help the government get reelected. Mr Blair is confusing our interests with his own.

The confusion may be systematic. It is easy for a politician convinced of his merit to conflate his own interests with those of the people. What could be better for the people than to be led by a great man or a virtuous political party? Anything that serves the interests of such a man or party thereby serves the interests of the people. Policies that are aimed solely at keeping New Labour in power must be, at least indirectly, in our best interests.

It is a preposterous view, but sometimes Mr Blair says things that suggest it. When cajoling the Labour Party to embrace his Third Way policies, the principle benefit he claimed for them was that they would get Labour elected. Never mind that these were precisely the policies that all in the Labour Party, including Mr Blair, had recently insisted were calamitous for society. What matters is not the policies themselves but who implements them. Policies that were wicked under the Conservatives are blessed when taken over by Labour. What Britain needs is a Labour government, whatever it does.

PART VI
Case Study

In this final part of the book I consider one of Mr Blair's speeches in its entirety. The speech I have chosen is 'Choice, Excellence and Equality', which he delivered at Guy's and St Thomas' Hospital in London on the 23rd of June 2004. Mr Blair's words are presented with my comments interspersed. Much could be said about this speech, but I restrict myself to points about its logical coherence and transparency.

Most of the fallacies in this speech have been covered in the preceding chapters. Where this is so, I simply identify the fallacy and give a chapter reference. Sometimes, however, Mr Blair makes a mistake to which I have not devoted a chapter and then I give a slightly fuller comment. Most often these new fallacies are simply *non sequiturs*: that is, Mr Blair claims that one proposition follows from another when it does not. I did not write a chapter about *non sequitur* because, although political rhetoric is full of it, there is nothing general you can say about *non sequitur*. It's just a brute mistake, like adding two and two and getting five.

Before considering the particular mistakes Mr Blair makes as he goes along, it is worth considering the speech as a whole. It is supposed to provide an overview and defence of Mr Blair's choice-based public services policies: the policies he means to implement in a third Labour term in government.

The most striking peculiarity of the speech, given this purpose, is that it says almost nothing about these policies. It is not until he is about three quarters of the way through the speech that Mr Blair explains a single policy in anything but the most vague and metaphorical terms. And at no point does he give any reason to think that his policies will succeed.

The day before the speech, the Prime Minister's Official Spokesman said that the speech would lay out Mr Blair's principles. Yet serious principles – ideas from economics that might explain how consumer choices of the kinds he proposes will improve the public services – are nowhere to be found. He relies solely on metaphors about 'tailor made' and 'personalised' services to make his proposals appear attractive.

The vast majority of the speech is devoted to telling the story of Britain's public services and describing the measures the Labour government has undertaken in recent years, especially its increased spending on health and education. Yet all of this is entirely beside the point. It helps neither explain Mr Blair's proposed new choice-based policies nor show why they are a good idea.

Choice, Excellence and Equality
Wednesday 23 June 2004

Over the coming three months, I will be setting out an agenda for a third term Labour Government. A major part of that agenda will be about the future of public services in health, education, law and order, transport, housing and employment. But the battle over public services is more than a battle about each individual service. **(False dichotomy, ch.9. What battle? With whom?)** The state of our public services defines the nature of our country. Our public realm is what we share together. How it develops tells us a lot about what we hold in common, the values that motivate us, the ideas that govern us. **(Highfalutin waffle, ch.1 and moral posturing, ch.2.)**

The New Labour Government was created out of the reform of progressive politics in Britain. For the first hundred years of our history as a party, we had been in government only intermittently. **(Irrelevant history, ch.8.)**

Our ambition was to govern in the way and manner of Labour in 1945 and the reforming Liberal Governments of the late 19th and early 20th century: **(Irrelevant favourable associations, ch.3.)** to construct a broad coalition of the better off and the less advantaged to achieve progress, economic and social, in the interests of the many not the few. **(Hooray words, ch.6.)**

In seven years, we have delivered a stable economy, rising employment, and big reductions in unemployment and poverty. **(Cum hoc ergo propter hoc fallacy, ch.13.)** With that behind us, we have invested in our public realm. In particular, we have systematically raised the capacity and quality of our public services. Over the last few months there has been a growing recognition and acceptance that real improvement is happening. **(Democratic fallacy, ch.7. In whom is this recognition growing?)**

Now, on the basis of this clear evidence of progress, is the time to accelerate reform. **(Non sequitur. Why should acceleration follow from clear evidence of progress? What is this evidence anyway?)**

In simple terms, we are completing the re-casting of the 1945 welfare state to end entirely the era of 'one size fits all' services and put in their place modern services which maintain at their core the values of equality of access and opportunity for all; base the service round the user, a personalised service with real choice, greater individual responsibility and high standards; and ensure in so doing that we keep our public services universal, for the middle class as well as those on lower incomes, both of whom expect and demand services of quality. **(Opaque metaphor, ch.5 and Hooray words, ch.6.)**

I am not talking about modest further reorganization but something quite different and more fundamental. We are proposing to put an entirely different dynamic in place to drive our public services: one where the service will be driven not by the government or by the managers but by the user – the patient, the parent, the pupil and the law abiding citizen.

(Opaque metaphor, ch.5.) The service will continue to be free, but it will be a high quality consumer service to fit their needs in the same way as the best services do in other areas of life. **(Promising the apparently impossible. See the discussion of this unpriced choice proposal in ch.12. Note also that taxpayers might object to the claim that public services are now free.)**

This is a vision which combines choice, excellence and equality in a modern universal welfare state. **(Hooray words, ch.6.)**

We will contrast such a vision with that of the Conservatives whose essential anti-public service ideology is shown by their policy to subsidise a few to opt-out of public services at the expense of the many; to abandon targets for public service performance; and to cut the overall amount of public spending drastically. **(False dichotomy, ch.9.)** There are frequent gyrations in their precise policies; but unchanging in each new version is that a privileged minority can and should opt out in order to get a better service. **(Straw man fallacy, ch.9.)**

By contrast, I believe the vast majority of those on centre-left now believe in the new personalised concept of public services. **(Elitist variation of the democratic fallacy, ch.7.)** It is true that some still argue that people – usually other people – don't want choice. That, for example, they just want a single excellent school and hospital on their doorstep.

In reality, I believe people do want choice, in public services as in other services. But anyway choice isn't an end in itself. It is one important mechanism to ensure that citizens can indeed secure good schools and health services in their communities. **(How does this mechanism work?)** And choice matters as much within those institutions as between them: better choice of learning options for each pupil within secondary schools; better choice of access routes into the health service. Choice puts the levers in the hands of parents and patients so that they as citizens and consumers can be a driving force for improvement in their public services. And the choice we support is choice open to all on the basis of their equal status as citizens not on the unequal basis of their wealth. **(Opaque metaphor, ch.5. What are these 'levers' with which parents and patients will become 'driving forces'? Will successful schools make profits and failures make losses? That's how it works in the private sector that Mr Blair seeks to emulate. How will that be achieved without pricing their services?)**

This is the case we will take to the British people. **(What case? None has been given!)** It is a case only possible because of our investment. Without investment in capacity and in essential standards and facilities, sustained not just for a year or two but year on year as a matter of central national purpose, there is no credibility in claims to be able to extend choice to all. They become mere words without meaning for the great majority of citizens, as demonstrated by the last government which promised these things but refused the investment in capacity and so ended up making its flagship policies on choice the assisted places scheme, a grammar school in every town, and subsidies for private health insurance; all of them opt-out policies for a small minority at the expense of the rest. **(False dichotomy, ch.8. Failings of the previous government cannot show that Mr Blair's policies will work; Non sequitur. How does 'opting out' cause expense to those who do not opt out?)**

Some propose to return to these policies. To return to choice for the few. To offer what is in effect not a right to choose but a right to charge. To constrain investment, either by directly cutting it or by siphoning it off money to subsidise those currently purchasing private provision. **(Gibberish. What does it mean to 'constrain investment by ...**

'siphoning it off money to subsidise those currently purchasing private provision'?)

Our goal is fundamentally different **(False dichotomy, ch.8.)** and more ambitious for the people of Britain and I will set it out today.

Let me go back to 1997 and describe our journey as a government. **(Irrelevant history, ch.8. Here begins many paragraphs telling a simplified story of Britain's public services. It neither clarifies nor justifies his proposed choice-based policies. They are a long and pointless digression.)**

We inherited public services in a state of widespread dilapidation – a claim almost no-one would deny. This wasn't because public services and their staff were somehow inferior; on the contrary, our health and education services had achieved about as much as it was possible to achieve on constrained budgets and decades of under-investment. The problem was too little resource, and therefore grossly inadequate capacity in terms of staff and facilities.

This under-investment was not tackled in the Eighties and into the Nineties, even as economic conditions allowed. On the contrary, it was maintained as an act of policy and philosophy right up until 1997. So in 1997 the hospital building programme had ground to a halt, despite a £3bn repairs backlog. Capital investment was at its lowest level for a decade. Waiting lists were rising at their fastest rate ever. Nurse training places had been cut by a quarter. Training places for GPs were cut by one fifth. In education, teacher numbers had fallen by 36,000 since 1981. Funding per pupil was actually cut by over £100 between 1992 and 1997. Police numbers were down by 1,100.

Underinvestment and chronic lack of capacity led, inevitably, to a failure to meet even basic standards. Standards not simply unmet, but undefined, for the simple reason that defining them would have demonstrated how far each public service was from achieving them.

(**The irrelevant history continues.**) So there was no national expectation of success at school for young people – although nearly half of 11 year-olds were not even up to standard in the basics of literacy and numeracy and a similar proportion left school at or soon after 16 with few if any qualifications.

There was no effective maximum waiting time either for a GP appointment or for hospital treatment – although the hospital waiting lists stood at over 1.1 million and many patients were waiting more than 18 months even for the most urgent treatment, with rates of death from cancer and heart disease amongst the highest in Europe.

There were no national targets for reducing crime or dealing with youth offending, though crime had doubled since 1979 and it was taking four and a half months to deal with young offenders from arrest to sentence. Community penalties were not properly enforced, fines were not paid.

And not only were none of these basic foundations in existence. Perhaps worse, there was a fatalism, cultivated assiduously by those opposed to public spending on ideological principle, that this was the natural order of things, that somehow there was a 'British disease' which meant we were culturally destined to have second-rate education and health and rising crime. (**The pointless history lecture continues.**) The nation with some of the best universities in the world somehow destined to have crumbling, substandard primary and secondary schools; the nation which under Labour founded the National Health Service in the 1940s – one of the great international beacons of the post-war era – still leaving patients on trolleys in corridors, with easily treatable conditions – hip and knee-joint replacements, cataracts – largely untreated because of lack of facilities.

Our first task in 1997, within an indispensable framework of economic stability and growth, was to invest in capacity; to herald public investment in education, health and law and order as a virtue not a curse; and to define basic standards and to reform working practices so that extra resources delivered real capacity improvements service by service. We did so with confidence and optimism. With confidence that public service staff – the doctors, teachers, police officers, and the vital ancillary staff of all kinds – would rise to this challenge, with the better pay, training and incentives they needed and deserved. **(Flattery and moral posturing, ch.2.)** And with optimism that they would bring abut radical improvement – not immediately; not until the resources and reform programmes on which they depended had started to make an impact; but in a sustained fashion once the real rates of investment – rising now to 7.5% a year in health and 6% a year in education – had begun to drive reform and build capacity.

Let me pause to say what that year on year investment means. **(Equivocation, ch.4. He calls an ongoing increase in government spending 'investment' to take advantage of investment's superior reputation.)** In health, it means a budget now doubled from £33bn in 1997 to £67bn this year, and set to rise to £90bn by 2008, bringing our health spending towards the European average for the first time in a generation. This is enabling us to recruit 20,000 more doctors, 68,000 more nurses and 26,000 more therapy, scientific and technical staff. **(Benefit Benefit analysis, ch.14. In the following paragraphs Mr Blair lists the benefits of his increased government spending. But he does not show that the benefits exceed the cost in increased taxation. Indeed, he doesn't even mention this cost.)** In education it means a budget nearly doubled, from £30bn to £53bn, again bringing us towards international standards with 29,000 extra teachers in our schools. In law and order it means a 25% real increase in police funding since 1999, and police numbers up 11,000. Across the public services, infrastructure being transformed – new buildings, ICT, equipment, facilities, in every locality in the country in ongoing programmes of investment. The schools capital programme, for example, up from £680m a year in 1997 to £4.5 billion a year today, enabling us to embark on a programme to bring every secondary school in the country – all 3,400 of them – up to a modern standard by 2015. A completely different physical environment for learning, transforming the potential of our teachers.

But money alone was never going to put even the basics right. We in government never tired of saying – alongside so many public service leaders themselves, frustrated at past failure – that it had to be money tied to reform to ensure that basic standards were defined and delivered in each service. The workforce had to be modernized as it was enlarged and better paid; basic standards and practices defined and delivered; rewards tied to service improvements; a new engagement with private and voluntary sectors; and full accountability to the public which was being asked to pay for the service improvements, with proper independent inspection and assessment.

So our policy was not simply smaller class sizes and more teachers – although we achieved both. **(Still the irrelevant history goes on! When will he get to the supposed topic of this speech: his plans for a third term in government?)** It was also literacy and numeracy programmes, building on best existing teaching practice, to raise basic standards systematically nationwide – 84,000 more 11 year-olds a year now up to standard in maths and 60,000 in English. It was a radical recasting of the teaching profession to embed teaching assistants alongside teachers and give them a defined role – now more than 130,000 of them, double the number in 1997. **(The benefit benefit analysis also continues, unsullied by the mention of any costs.)** It was a reform of secondary education – including Excellence in Cities and the specialist schools and academies programmes – tackling failing

schools systematically and embedding higher standards and
a culture of aspiration school by school. Substantial progress
is now evident on all fronts: the number of failing schools is
down, there is a new culture of achievement and expectation
in our secondary schools, and 50,000 more 16 year olds a year
now achieving five or more good GCSEs.

Similarly, our policy in heath was not simply more doctors, nurses and new buildings – although we have achieved
a step-change in all three. It was the first national system of
hospital inspection. The first national maximum waiting
times for GP appointments, hospital treatment and A&E.
New national service frameworks for treatment of cancer and
heart disease. Premature deaths from heart disease – the single biggest killer – are down by a quarter since 1997, with a
third more heart operations, twice as many patients receiving
immediate access to clot-busting drugs and cholesterol lowering drugs now prescribed to 1.8 million people. **(And on he
goes with the irrelevance. Time is running out. Get to the
point!)**

The statistics don't of course tell the real story of lives
saved and transformed. Take, for example, the family turning
up at A & E with their elderly relative who has fallen at
home.

Before the investment and reforms now in place they
would most likely have faced a long and worrying wait, probably in a shabby casualty department. They would have read
the stories about 'waiting 48 hours on a trolley in a corridor'
and expected the same.

Today, their elderly relative will be seen and treated within
4 hours at the very most, but typically much quicker. There
will be more staff in the A & E than previously and the facilities will very likely have been refurbished with play areas
for children and so on.

In law and order, too, it is a similar story of bold statistics proclaiming real change – not only the 11,000 extra police, but also 3,300 community support officers where this type of role simply didn't exist in 1997. **(Yet more benefit benefit analysis. These extra police aren't free. How do we know they are worth it?)** Overall crime, according to the British Crime Survey, down by 4 million incidents a year, with the blight of burglary down to its lowest level for over 20 years.

This week we held a reception at No 10 for front-line staff. **(Moral posturing, ch.2. Receptions for front-line staff! Man of the people.)** Many of them were people whose jobs didn't even exist seven years ago. New Deal advisers who have helped cut youth unemployment to a few thousand nation-wide. Sure Start workers. Nurse consultants. Community Support Officers. NHS Direct staff. Classroom assistants. All of them giving us the capacity to help thousands upon thousands in new ways. **(Benefit benefit analysis. Why should we be glad that these new jobs have been created? Are Community Support Officers worth what they cost?)**

So, taking stock, we have raised capacity to a new plateau. And it is from this plateau that we can climb to the next vital stage of public reform, to design and provide truly personal-ized services, meeting the needs and aspirations of today's generation for choice, quality and opportunity service by service on which to found their lives and livelihoods. **(Opaque metaphors, ch.5 and hooray words, ch.6. But at least the history seems to be finished.)**

Choice and diversity are not somehow alien to the spirit of the public services – or inconsistent with fairness. **(Whoever said choice and fairness were inconsistent? 'Tea or Coffee?' 'How unfair!', ch.12.)**

The reason too many of the public services we inherited were stuck in the past, in terms of choice and quality – and the two or even more tiers of service they offered – was be-cause their funding, infrastructure and service standards were stuck in the past too. **(Variation on hooray words, ch.6. Boo words: 'Stuck in the past.' Sounds bad but what does it mean? Perhaps it only means that you disagree with Mr Blair's proposals.)**

Back in the 1940s, **(Oh no! We're slipping back in time again. Mr Blair seems to be stuck in the past.)** the public services were top-down in their management – like so much else at the time, and this remained too entrenched thereafter. But they were every bit as good as the private sector in terms of choice and quality – if not far better, particularly after the 1944 Education Act and the founding of the NHS, which offered services and opportunities transformed from the pre-war years within a post-war economy and society governed by rationing, funding constraints, and pervasive low skills and aspirations. Aneurin Bevan said the NHS civilized the country. **(Irrelevant positive associations, ch.3.)** It extended choice, quality and opportunity in its generation: it didn't limit them. And when it came to means rather than ends, Bevan was entirely pragmatic about how provision should be funded and structured within the new NHS, consistent with its values of equality and fairness. **(Hooray words, ch.6.)**

The following decades saw a growing divergence between the availability of choice – and the perception and often the reality of quality – between the public and private sectors. But on the basis of the new plateau of capacity, we can change that, whilst keeping intact the ethos of public service. **(Hooray words, ch.6. What is the 'ethos of public service'? How will we know if it is still intact?)**

Choice and quality will be for all – driven by extra capacity, without charges or selection by wealth. **(What is 'selection by wealth'? Do supermarkets and lawyers, who charge for their goods and services, commit this crime?)**

In health, we will set out tomorrow a new guarantee of treatment within a set time which starts from the moment a patient is referred by their GP – not the time that they get onto the queue for their operation. Every patient will have a right to be seen and treated within this period, with a choice of which provider undertakes the treatment. **(Finally, at the three quarter mark, a clear statement of something Mr Blair is proposing!)**

In education, we want every parent to be able to choose a good secondary school. So we are providing for every secondary school to become a specialist school, with a centre of excellence in one part of the curriculum; **(Non sequitur. How does giving every parent access to a specialist school guarantee that they will have access to a good school?)** and to raise aspiration and achievement in areas where the education system has failed in the past, we will expand the number of academies significantly. We will also reform the curriculum so that students get a better and broader range of options for study beyond the age of 14, developing their talents and challenging them to achieve more.

In law and order, we will re-introduce community policing for today's age with dedicated policing teams of officers and community support officers focused on local priorities, implementing tough new powers to deal with anti-social behaviour. **(Hooray words, ch.6. 'For today's age.' Hooray! We don't want policies for yesterday's age.)** There will also be personalised support for every victim of crime as we introduce a new witness care service nationwide. **(Opaque metaphor, ch.5. How do these policies embody Mr Blair's earlier claim that law abiding citizens will drive the criminal justice system?)**

The same principles will be extended across the public services. In social housing, for example, we will extend choice-based lettings – which give council and housing association tenants a new service to identify locations and properties, in place of traditional schemes where tenants were simply allocated a property on the basis of a centrally-imposed points system. **(Promising the apparently impossible, ch.12. How will central allocation be avoided when every applicant will choose the best social housing?)**

In welfare, every person of working age able to work – wherever they live and whatever their needs – will receive personalised support, including personal advisers able to provide tailored support to help people back into work, not just registered job seekers but steadily more of the three million of working age who are otherwise economically inactive. **(Hooray words, ch.6. How do personal advisers differ from impersonal ones? What is Mr Blair really proposing here? Why is it a good idea?)**

As we accelerate reform on the basis of enhanced capacity, these personalized services will be made available in every community.

Over the last seven years New Labour has time and again shown how ideas that are supposed to be irreconcilable can be brought together: social justice and economic efficiency; fairness at work and a flexible labour market; full employment and low inflation. **(Bogus claim to have overcome old trade-offs, ch.12.)**

It is the same with choice, excellence and equity. There is no reason except past failure why excellence need mean elitism – why there can only be good schools and universities if a majority are kept out of them; why there can only be real choice and diversity if a majority are deprived of them. With the right services, expectations and investment, we can have excellence for the great majority, with choice and equity. And we don't base this on theory, but on what is now happening in practice. **(False dichotomy, ch.9. Mr Blair here appears to be arguing against some imaginary and very stupid adversary.)**

Consider healthcare, where we have now been trialling

choice in the public services for a number of years. The evidence shows there is demand for choice and that this is not only compatible with equity but that choice itself helps to ensure equity.

In the NHS there have been trials in elective surgery with patients offered a choice of up to four hospitals for treatment, often assisted by a Patient Care Adviser. Take-up is high.

Half of all those offered a choice of where to have their heart operation in the nationwide cardiac scheme took up the offer. More than two thirds of patients offered a choice in the London trial took up the offer. Three quarters did so in Manchester. (**As presented, this statement is impossible to understand. When I am presented with a choice, I must reject all but one of my options. But how can I reject the choice itself. Whichever option I take, I have made a choice.**)

The schemes have had a dramatic effect on waiting times. In the London pilot, extending patient choice led to a decrease in waiting times of 17% (compared with a 6% fall nationally). (**This appears to be a relevant observation. The speech was not a complete waste of time.**)

The recruitment of overseas suppliers into the NHS – setting up new treatment centres extending choice – has also had a significant effect. As the FT put it a fortnight ago: 'By introducing a clutch of overseas providers ... to provide treatment centres for National Health Service patients, the government has at a stroke transformed a significant chunk of the country's health care ... exposing to scrutiny some of the myths on which private medical care is sold.'

Greater choice and diversity are having a similarly positive effect in education and childcare. Our new under-fives provision – Sure Start, nursery places for three and four year-olds, better maternity and paternity support, a massive extension of childcare supported by tax credits – is enabling parents to choose the provision that is best for them and their children, where previously there was often no provision at all. (**It is stretching things to claim that guaranteed nursery places is an example of choice-based public services policies. Primary and secondary school places have always been guaranteed. Why then do we not already have the choice Mr Blair wants?**) It is also giving parents much greater flexibility in their working life, where previously they often had none, or indeed little incentive to work at all.

In secondary education, specialist schools have shown significant improvements in results, (**Almost all schools have shown significant improvements in results. National GCSE and A-level results have improved every year for twenty years.**) and most secondary schools and are now exploring the best curriculum areas in which to develop real centres of excellence and boost their provision. We have made it far easier for successful and popular schools to expand where they wish to do so, including special capital grants for new premises. New secondary school curriculum options, including junior apprenticeships for 14 to 16 year-olds, are giving pupils more choice to meet their aspirations, and we will take curriculum reform further. Academies are offering a wholly new type of independent state school, serving the whole community in areas where better provision is needed, and are proving popular. I have opened two of the new academies in the past year; it is truly remarkable what is possible when investment, aspiration and inspirational leadership – not tied down by past failure – go hand in hand. (**Moral posturing, ch.2. Mr Blair may be an inspirational leader but such boasting is unseemly.**)

Let me return to my starting point. With growing capacity in our public services we can now accelerate reform. We have the opportunity to develop a new generation of personalised services where equity and excellence go hand in hand – services shaped by the needs of those who use them, services with more choice extended to everyone and not just those that can afford to pay, services personal to each and fair to all. **(Hooray words, ch.6.)**

It is now accepted by all the political parties that the economy and public services will be the battleground at the next election. That in itself is a kind of tribute to what has been achieved. The territory over which we will fight is the territory we have laid out. **(Non sequitur. Why would the opposition choose to campaign on issues where the government has been as successful as Mr Blair claims to have been? Surely they pick on the government's weak spots.)**

For our part, we must fight it with a boldness no longer born out of instinct but of experience. When we have refused to accept the traditional frontiers but have gone beyond them, we have always found more fertile land. **(Highfalutin waffle, ch.1.)**

And there is another reason for approaching our task in this way: the world keeps changing ever faster. With the change comes new possibilities and new insecurities. It is always our job to help realise the one and overcome the other; to provide opportunity and security in this world of change; and for all, not for a few. **(Highfalutin waffle, ch.1 and hooray words, ch.6.)**

(And to finish, a recap of the irrelevant history and a flurry of grandiose waffle.) Take a step back and analyse seven years of this Government. Setbacks aplenty, for sure. But also real and tangible achievement and progress for many who otherwise would have been kept down, unable to realise their potential, without much hope and with little prospect of advance. Now we have to take it further: always with an eye to the future, always maintaining the coalition of the decent and the disadvantaged that got us here, always recognising that in politics if you aren't adventurous, you may never know failure, but neither are you likely to be acquainted with success.

There is still much to do and we intend to do it.

Endnotes

1. *Seven Pillars of a Decent Society*, Southampton, 16 April 1997.
2. *Seven Pillars of a Decent Society*.
3. *The Daily Express*, 9 October 2001.
4. *Seven Pillars of a Decent Society*.
5. *Labour Party Manifesto, 2001*, page 20. Top-up fees allow some universities to charge higher than normal tuition fees. Under the legislation passed, these fees can be up to £3,000 a year.
6. *Labour Party Manifesto, 2001*, page 10.
7. *Choice, Excellence and Equality*, Guy's and St Thomas' Hospital, London, 23 June 2004.
8. The original source of this much discussed story is Bob Woodward, *The Choice*, Touchstone 1997.
9. This was reported in the *Daily Mail*, 11 November 2002. According to Nick Cohen in *The Observer*, 8 December 2002, Number 10 did not deny the story when he inquired about its truth and the *Daily Mail* received no complaint from the Blairs or Number10.

10. *Seven Pillars of a Decent Society*. The idea that many British children live in poverty does not occur in this speech alone: it was an abiding theme in Mr Blair's early rhetoric. Now he claims that many children have been saved from poverty by his government.
11. Mr Blair used this expression to describe himself in November 1997. He was responding to critics who suspected that Formula One racing's special exemption from the government's ban on tobacco advertising at sports events might be connected to the fact that Bernie Eccleston, the owner of Formula One, had recently donated £1 million to the Labour Party.
12. *Choice, Excellence and Equality*.
13. 'This is not about tyranny, it's about freedom and security', *Daily Telegraph*, 4 May 2004.
14. 'Talking Euro-nonsense in the war for hearts and bottoms', *Daily Telegraph*, 7 May 2004.
15. 2004 Labour Party Conference speech.
16. *Seven Pillars of a Decent Society*.
17. Speech on the launch of the 5-year strategy for crime, 19 July 2004.
18. *Choice, Excellence and Equality*.
19. Speech on the economy, Napier University, Edinburgh, 3 December 2004.
20. 'Freedom Is Not Enough', *The Spectator*, 13 March 2004.
21. Quoted in 'Six Years to Bring the NHS Up to Scratch', *Daily Telegraph*, 17 January 2000.
22. Speech to the IPPR and Universities UK joint conference on higher education reform, 14 January 2004.
23. *Seven Pillars of a Decent Society*.
24. See for example Mr Blair's speech, *Values and the Power of Community*, to the Global Ethics

Foundation, Tübingen University, Germany, 30 June
2000.
25. 'A Referendum: Brave, Right and Risky', *Daily
Telegraph*, 19 April 2004.
26. *John* 1:1.
27. *Choice, Excellence and Equality*.
28. He revealed this policy, for example, during his press
briefing on the 30 April 2003.
29. *Newsnight*, BBC2, 17 May 2002.
30. 'Labour is hounding no one', *Daily Telegraph*, 20
September 1999.
31. 'Grown Up Politics for an Adult World', *The
Observer*, 21 November 2004.
32. *Seven Pillars of a Decent Society*.
33. 'Grown Up Politics for an Adult World', *The
Observer*, 21 November 2004.
34. Quoted in *The Times*, 19 November 2004.
35. *Panorama Leadership Special*, BBC1, 7 April 1997.
36. *Choice, Excellence and Equality*.
37. *Choice, Excellence and Equality*.
38. *Seven Pillars of a Decent Society*.
39. *Matthew* 16:28.
40. *Choice, Excellence and Equality*.
41. I owe this analysis to Anatole Kaletske in *The Times*,
26 August 2004.
42. *Choice, Excellence and Equality*.
43. In 1997 tax revenues were £315bn, which is about
£360bn in 2004 money.
44. Reported in the *Daily Telegraph*, 25 April 2001.
45. Reported in the *Guardian*, 16 August 2004.